# TRAPLINES AND TRAILS

A Book of Master
Trapping Methods

By
E. J. DAILEY

THE HUNTER-TRADER-TRAPPER CO.
COLUMBUS, OHIO, U. S. A.

ON THE TRAPLINE IN THE NORTHWEST

Copyrighted 1925

By

THE HUNTER-TRADER-TRAPPER
Columbus, Ohio.

All Rights Reserved.

FOURTH EDITION

Printed in the United States of America

# CONTENTS

| Chapter | | Page |
|---|---|---|
| Introduction | | 11 |
| 1. | Trapping Grounds—Fur Prospecting | 13 |
| II. | The Trapper's Habitation | 24 |
| III. | Equipment and Food | 33 |
| IV. | Things Every Trapper Should Know | 43 |
| V. | Adirondack Trapping | 52 |
| VI. | The Auto Trapline | 60 |
| VII. | The Fox | 65 |
| VIII. | The Skunk and How to Trap It | 82 |
| IX. | The Mink | 94 |
| X. | The Sly Otter | 106 |
| XI. | The Bear | 114 |
| XII. | The Busy Beaver | 121 |
| XIII. | The Muskrat | 129 |
| XIV. | The Raccoon | 144 |
| XV. | "Cats" | 155 |
| XVI. | The Marten | 163 |
| XVII. | The Weasel | 171 |
| XVIII. | Fisher and Wolverine | 181 |
| XIX. | The Elusive Wolf | 189 |
| XX. | Miscellaneous Fur-Bearers | 198 |
| XXI. | Incidents on the Trapline | 204 |
| XXII. | Under Ice and Other Trapping | 211 |
| XXIII. | The Care and Marketing of Furs | 218 |
| XXIV. | Fur Farming | 225 |
| XXV. | Outdoor Photography | 232 |
| Conclusion | | 239 |

# LIST OF ILLUSTRATIONS

|  | PAGE |
|---|---|
| On the Trapline in the Northwest | Frontispiece |
| Looking Under an Old Bridge for Fur Signs | 14 |
| A New York State Guide on a Hunting and Fur Prospecting Trip | 17 |
| A Trapping Stream in the Farmland Region | 20 |
| Good Trapping Grounds in New Ontario, Canada | 23 |
| The Best Type of Trapper's Habitation | 26 |
| The Bark Covered Camp is One of the Most Comfortable for Cold Regions | 29 |
| A Hastily Constructed Lean-to and a Porky for Dinner | 36 |
| The Type of Trapper Who Traps All Season but Never Buys any Traps | 46 |
| Searching for Mink Signs in the Deep Forest | 51 |
| A Good Mink and Otter Stream in the Adirondacks | 55 |
| A Trapper's Cabin with Mountainous Surroundings | 57 |
| A Spot Trapper | 62 |
| Fox Set in Animal Trail, Trap Uncovered | 67 |
| Good Fox Country | 70 |
| A Fox That Was Not Sly Enough | 73 |
| The Author with a Trapped Fox | 77 |
| Some Trappers Drag the Carcass of Certain Animals to Lure Fur-Bearers to Their Traps | 85 |
| A Striped Kitty Out for an Evening Stroll | 90 |
| Dailey with a Trapped Mink | 95 |
| A Mink Mixed up with a Trap | 98 |
| Making a Set in the End of a Partly Submerged Log | 101 |
| Trapped Mink | 103 |
| Making an Otter Set | 108 |
| Entrances to Den Used by Otter | 111 |
| Bruin Takes a Drink | 117 |
| Shooting a Trapped Beaver | 123 |
| Trees Cut by Beaver | 128 |
| Muskrat House in Good Trapping Section | 131 |
| Setting a Trap in a Run Used by Rats | 134 |
| On the Trail of the Muskrat | 137 |

## ILLUSTRATIONS

|  | PAGE |
|---|---|
| Spring Rat Skins | 139 |
| Removing a Trapped Rat | 142 |
| Looking Over a Den Coon Tree | 146 |
| At the Base of Large Trees is a Good Set Location | 151 |
| Two Lynx Manicuring Their Claws | 157 |
| Camp Used by Trappers and Hunters | 160 |
| A Simple Marten Set | 164 |
| Trap Set at a Bait Pen | 166 |
| Hollow Tree Sets are Used for Marten | 168 |
| Baited Weasel Set | 174 |
| Trapped Weasel | 178 |
| On the Trapline in Winter | 183 |
| A Trapper's Line Camp in the Rockies | 186 |
| Green Timber, the Haunt of Fisher, Marten and Lynx | 188 |
| Trapped Coyote | 192 |
| The Author in Front of His Adirondack Camp | 197 |
| Tree in the Distance Used as a Den by Coon | 200 |
| Taking a Shot at Game | 207 |
| Evergreen in Winter | 214 |
| Some Farmland Furs | 220 |
| Silver Fox on a Fur Farm | 227 |
| A Lady Trapper and Deer She Killed | 235 |
| E. J. Dailey with "Go Light Camping Outfit" | 240 |

# Traplines and Trails

# INTRODUCTION

"A trapper is never known by the length of his trapline, nor by the number of traps he uses, but by the pelts that adorn his cabin wall."—DAILEY.

TRAPPING, and the business of fur-trading, is considered the oldest industry in America. The very existence of our forefathers depended on these vocations. It was attended with grave dangers at that time, yet apparently the carefree life suited the majority of these conquerors of the New World.

This happened many hundred years ago, yet the "call of the trails," and the longing for a life in the open, has been handed down from generation to generation, and today, it exists in our hearts just as strongly as it did in the hearts of our ancestors of centuries ago. Therefore, friends of the trail and trapline, we must remember that our children and our children's children, will feel the same longing to pursue the haunters of the wild, that you and I have felt, and it is up to us to do our part, so that there will be an everlasting continuation of trapping. An old Adirondack guide, who has long since, taken the one way trail, once said: "These wild things are not ours to do as we like with, but were given us in trust, and we must answer for them to the coming generations."

The conservation of our wild animal life is of the greatest importance. Take this away in its entirety, and our fair land would be as devoid of human interest as the most barren parts of a desert.

Fundamentally, this book was written to aid those of the trapping fraternity, yet I trust that no reader will ever try to trap out the last fur-bearing dwellers of his trapping domain, but will cease to pursue, the moment they show scarceness. Do not trap too early or continue late in the season, and protect the animals at all other times. If a wise fur-bearer evades your set, do not be angry, for it is the chance that makes trapping the "sport of the most thrills."

I am confident that with good, enforced game laws, and a general understanding among trappers that seed must always be saved if there is to be a future crop, that trapping and the great fur industry will continue indefinitely.

There are four practices which have more to do with reducing our fur supply than all others. They are: (1) Destroying dens which leave the animals with no suitable places to rear their young. (2) Trapping late in the Spring which destroys females with young. (3) Trapping early in the Fall which takes many young, unsuspicious fur-bearers, which have little value as the fur is thin and unmatured. (4) Using poison which kills many animals that are never found and even continues its deadly work long after the trapping season has closed.

Catch all the prime skins you can, but play square with the animals.—Dailey.

# CHAPTER I

## TRAPPING GROUNDS—FUR PROSPECTING

WHERE are the best trapping grounds? is the commonest question asked by the entire trapping fraternity. Almost every American trapper is planning on new and better grounds where the elusive citizens of the wild, visits one's traps with regularity. The Southern toe-pincher dreams of the Northern realm, where wolves and other roamers of the silences howl around the cabin door, and the Northerner, half frozen by fifty below zero weather, and with his entire trapline covered by three feet of snow, longs for the land where he could tend a trapline all winter through with no mittens or great coat. But longing and planning is about as far as the most trappers ever get, and year after year they ply the same old lines or add loops, and all the time gaining knowledge regarding the things of the great outdoors. Many trappers who plan on going into the mountains and woods to make a living and more pursuing the sly fur-bearing dwellers of those sections, have had so little experience in the vocation of trapping that they failed to make good in the home section where 'rats, skunks, and other easily taken animals were fairly plentiful. A trapper who cannot catch foxes on his local grounds need not try to catch the more wary foxes and other slippery, nocturnal travelers of the backwoods places.

LOOKING UNDER AN OLD BRIDGE FOR FUR SIGNS

However if a trapper has started in at the bottom and has studied the trapping game thoroughly, and can trap the common fur-bearers successfully, he is in position to go in for something on a larger scale. It is a good plan for a trapper going into a strange section of the country to be prepared in the way of funds so that if he fails the first season, he can still continue for another. Many trappers that I have known personally, made a rank failure the first year they worked new grounds, and later picked up a small fortune. I am not one to knock my own vocation. Nearly every trapper advises others to keep out of the business. This may be natural, as they do not welcome competition. Yet these same persons keep on at the business to the very end. True, it is no get-rich-quick proposition at the best, and there are many hardships to be encountered. Yet during considerable travel among trappers I find them in very good circumstances, and above all, happy, and surely health and happiness are greater assets than all the wealth in the world. Here in the Adirondack region, I know of trappers who make fifteen hundred dollars each year, and what man has done, man may do. I have taken five hundred dollars value of muskrats in one month, and I know of a trapper in New York State that caught seven hundred dollars' worth of beaver during the month of March, 1925. I am of course citing the high spots, but every occupation has its failures. A person to be a successful trapper must be energetic, observing, and not easily discouraged. I have traveled over long trails and traplines for a week with but a few paltry skins of the least valuable fur-bearers to my credit, and yet in one day at a later date, picked up two hundred dollars' worth of furs.

If you are not satisfied with local conditions, by all means go out and search for new grounds. If you find what suits you, you are surely ahead, and if you do not, it may raise your opinion of the grounds you left to the extent that you will be satisfied to continue over the same old trails.

### GOOD TRAPPING SECTIONS

When a trapper decides to look for new trapping grounds, he usually purchases a few dozen maps, and notes the parts that have the most streams, ponds, woods, and mountains. From a monetary standpoint, he would be better off locating the great marshes, where muskrat, 'coon, and mink abound. Michigan, Maryland, New Jersey, New York, and Louisiana have the best marsh territories, but there is good marsh and lowland trapping in almost every State and the Southern part of Canada. Some sections go in for muskrat propagation, and much of the best territory is posted against trapping, as regards outside trappers. These 'rat farmers depend on hiring trappers during the trapping season, but one must be able to bring in the skins to command real wages. This is just as much a fact in every other vocation. There are plenty of good sections available at the present which are ideal for fur farming, so if your old grounds have played out and the remaining fur-bearers need a chance to propagate to the extent where trapping will pay once more, look up a marsh or stream and rent or buy it. Then do not trap

A NEW YORK STATE GUIDE ON A HUNTING AND
FUR PROSPECTING TRIP

close for a year or two and you have a yearly income guaranteed, and the very work you are most adapted to. Muskrat farms must be enclosed with wire and it must extend below the ground as well as somewhat above. Of course one loses what 'rats that would come on to his territory by fencing, even while he keeps in those that were there and what are raised.

The great wilderness sections of the States lie in Arizona, New Mexico, Northern California, Oregon, Washington, Michigan, Maine, New York, Minnesota, South Dakota, Oklahoma, South Carolina, and Wyoming. The provinces of Canada that have the most wild sections are British Columbia, New Ontario, Northern Manitoba, Alberta, and Saskatchewan. Some parts of Quebec have vast woods sections.

New Ontario probably contains more waste land and strictly wilderness tracts than any of the others. From North Bay, nearly to Winnipeg, a distance of more than five hundred miles, the region is almost a trackless wilderness. A few mining towns are to be found, where silver is taken from the great masses of granite and quartz. The country on every side is timbered with spruce, fir, cedar, and poplar. With few settlers and inadequate fire protection, terrible forest fires have devastated great territories, which however, quickly grew up to scrub poplar and other brush. This thick brushy territory makes good hiding and food for countless deer, while moose, bear, and other larger game are to be found in many sections. For fur-bearers there are marten, fisher, lynx, fox, and most of the lesser kinds common to the North. This is a terrible cold

Province, and much colder than some of the extreme Western Provinces, which receive a little warmth from the Pacific winds. The Northern part of New Ontario will compare favorably with Alaska, as to weather conditions. Snow usually arrives in October or even earlier and remains until May. Other parts of the Province will not differ much from the mountainous regions of the Northern part of the States.

A citizen of the States who contemplates going into Canada will be obliged to pay a license fee of about fifty dollars each year, depending on the Province, and in some instances, a royalty on all fur taken. Alaska, which is practically a part of the United States, offers about as much in the way of trapping, with a cheaper license. If one intends to take up Canadian trapping seriously, and he is a resident of the States, he should take up land in that country and take out papers proving his allegiance to the King. A license may then be procured at citizen's rates.

Wonderful trapping grounds where fur-bearers die of natural causes, are only to be found in small territories which are known to the trapping fraternity as "fur pockets." These pockets are located in every state and province, and every hustling trapper may locate one or more if he has the nerve to keep looking.

### FUR PROSPECTING

A trapper that does not keep on the line the entire year is not a trapper in the real sense of the word. One cannot work at some other vocation the summer through, and expect to compete with the

A TRAPPING STREAM IN THE FARMLAND REGION

trapper who has been keeping in close touch with the fur-bearers on his regular line, as well as looking up new and better locations.

The early part of the summer can be spent in locating where the young animals are being raised, knowing that they will invariably return to the old den during the fall. After September first, one should be locating new trapping grounds and prospecting for furs.

Fur prospecting is one of the greatest arts of the vocation of trapping. When snow is on the ground and tracks may be recognized, the amount of fur-dwellers in a section is easily known, but in the early autumn, when the leaves are falling, one must be adept at sign reading, to tell a good trapping territory from a poor one. Slight scratches on trees, or the banks of streams tell a story to the expert as plainly as though it were written in a book. A hiking outfit is essential to the welfare of a fur prospector. Most of the prospecting is done in remote places where no roads or even trails are to be found, therefore one must pack his food and outfit with him. A strip of canvas known as a tarp, will answer for a shelter, and the food should be of the highly concentrated kinds, as no extra weight should be carried. Dried foods are the best, and cans should usually be dispensed with.

When prospecting for fur-bearers, one should keep the fact in mind that natural food has more to do with the plentifulness of animals in any territory than any one other factor. Dens, feeding-grounds, and trails must all be located, if one wishes to be in a position to get his traps out quickly when the season arrives.

Along streams are ideal places to look for signs of every animal, for the land fur-bearers visit the streams often, and there are usually soft, muddy places where imprints of the feet may be located. It is not a good plan to prospect for wilderness fur-bearers close to regions where lumbering is in operation. Foxes are the only animals that hang around lumber camps, and they do this, apparently knowing that there are sure to be horses killed on steep inclines, and a dead horse means a winter's food for a fox.

Often a trip over a section that has been abandoned as useless by trappers, will surprise the prospector in the amount of fur signs located. Animals migrate to untrapped territory, and even grounds that were devoid of fur one season may be very good within a few years.

A trapper should not undertake to make a living on any strange trapping ground, without first prospecting it thoroughly, for I have known very good looking grounds to contain such a small percentage of fur-bearers, that one could make nothing. This could be caused by too close trapping previously, or scarcity of food.

When looking for muskrats in a marshy section, one can determine about the correct amount of animals during the fall, by multiplying the number of freshly built houses by five. 'Rats in a marsh section or in a swamp will leave more sign than on a stream. This is partly due to the fact that the running water, which is usually rising or lowering, eliminates much of the telltale marks.

A good map is useful to a fur prospector. The government topographical maps for sale at a rea-

TRAPLINES AND TRAILS 23

sonable rate by the Biological Survey, Washington, D. C., cover almost every section in the States, and are made on a very good scale for trapping and prospecting purposes.

GOOD TRAPPING GROUNDS IN NEW ONTARIO, CANADA

## CHAPTER II

## THE TRAPPER'S HABITATION

### LOG CABINS

THE log cabin is the standard of America, when it comes to choosing a camp for a trapper's dwelling. In a few sections, other types of camps are more in general use, but having experienced the use of nearly every kind, I can truthfully say that for comfort and convenience, no other style of trapper's habitation equals the cabin of logs. The longer I follow the vocation of trapping, the more I appreciate genuine comfort in camps and equipment. As an amateur, I used to think I was not a real outdoorsman unless I withstood many hardships. I have taken long trips in cold weather with no other equipment than one blanket, a fry pan, a belt axe, and a gun. I've frozen by the side of smoky camp fires, been half drowned in hastily constructed lean-tos, when a big rain came up, and I've been baked one minute and frozen the next, in improperly heated tents. Later I came to realize that a real woodsman always sought comfort in preference to everything else, and a well-built log cabin will give its owner more satisfactory service than any other camp. A framed dwelling, sheeted and papered is of course just as preferable, but the material for building such camp is seldom available, while logs and chinking are nearly always to be found in "the trapper's country."

The size of the proposed cabin will be determined by the number of persons intending to occupy it. Two trappers work together more than any other number, although many far back toe-pinchers play a "lone hand." Fifteen by eighteen feet is amply large for ordinary requirements of two trappers for a headquarters camp. The easiest type to build is the shanty-roof style. Some builders get the proper slope by working in logs near the top that are smaller at one end, and placing the large ends next the front. A gable roof is more satisfactory and gives more room. I heartily advise that whenever possible, roofing paper be used for a roof covering, but where this cannot be procured, shingles should be split from soft, straight-grained, wood like cedar or white pine. Bark slabs are next best, and where nothing else is obtainable, earth may be used. When the last mentioned substance is made use of, the pitch should be greater than with the others. Earth works very well in a snow country or even during rains if it has lain long enough for a covering of grass to accumulate.

For heating the cabin, a good stove is considered best, but if too far back to get in this requisite, a fireplace must be substituted. This can be made of flat stones and may be filled in with wet, yellow clay, which will turn to brick when burned. The space in the chimney should be partly filled in a zig-zag manner when placing the stones, so that the smoke can escape, but the heat be held back. The fireplace should be placed at one end of the cabin, and usually is made with one half inside and the other out. This saves room if nothing else.

Door material can be split out of logs and pinned

THE BEST TYPE OF TRAPPER'S HABITATION

together if necessary, but a few large nails save much time and labor. The skin of a large animal is sometimes framed for a door.

Many cabins are built with no means of lighting other than what filters down the fireplace chimney. A sheet of transparent celluloid, which is easily procured in any large town is easily packed in and makes fine illumination for a log cabin. A piece of white duck will suffice, and glass best of all when obtainable.

One should pick a sheltered spot when building a cabin, but not close to very large trees that might be blown down in a storm. The question of storm winds must influence the locating of any camp, and natural shelter should be provided on the side where the hardest storms come from.

For overnight trapping camps, a small shanty-type cabin will suffice. The smaller it is, the easier heated. Logs about eight inches through are large enough for this purpose. Moss is more universally used for chinking than any other one material. Earth or sod is sometimes used, and wet leaves a poor substitute.

### THE LEAN-TO

Open camps and particularly the lean-to is used to some extent by trappers from the Ozarks to the Hudson Bay. Some trappers and others spend entire winters in them where the temperature hovers at forty below for months at a time. The real use of the open camp, however, is for overnight shelter when caught out in the woods. They will suffice for fur-prospecting or other early fall camps. Logs make the best open camps, and those from eight to twelve inches through should be selected. As for a regular cabin, only straight ones should be selected, and dead trees are lighter to handle than live ones. They must be notched in a V-shape for the back corners and one or two logs are often laid the whole way around for strength. The others will need pinning with long wooden pins at the front. What has been said regarding roofing of cabins will apply to permanent lean-tos.

For overnight shelter only, evergreen boughs are used extensively for both siding and roof. A frame is made by placing a pole from one crotched tree to another, and then other poles laid from this to the ground. Then boughs are piled on the top and leaned up on the sides. The ground may be covered with evergreen boughs also. Like other types this camp is heated by reflection. If it cannot be built facing a natural reflector, one should be built of green logs a few feet in front of the camp. The fire is then built between the logs and the camp. These open camps are used by some of the Indians of the far North and are known as puckivans or Siwash camps. At their best, they are apt to be smoky and uncomfortable. Just a point better than the outdoors.

### TENTS

For moving from one place to another, nothing equals a tent, and they can be used for all year habitations with a fair degree of comfort. For the auto trapper or other type of the so-called "spot trapper," the tent is the thing.

Unlike the cabin, a rather large size is invariably more comfortable than a small one. This is due to

THE BARK COVERED CAMP IS ONE OF THE MOST COMFORTABLE FOR COLD REGIONS

the fact that they do not get hot so quickly nor cool down so fast. For permanent or semi-permanent use a tent should be provided with a sod cloth and a "fly." It should also be banked with leaves or other material.

In a deep snow country, an extra roof should be built of poles as a heavy snowfall raises havoc with a tent. A small stove is best for heating and is usually placed at the front of the tent so that the pipe can be extended to the outside. The stovepipe should be higher than the tent to prevent smoking. A screen should be placed in the upper end to prevent sparks from burning the tent or other surroundings. I consider a wall tent of the regulation pattern to excel all others, and a twelve by fourteen will accommodate four persons. For the auto trapper that moves every day, a wedge or miner's style tent will suffice. For fur prospecting when the outfit has to be carried, silk tents are much lighter than drill or duck. I have never seen an untreated tent that was absolutely waterproof unless used in connection with a fly. If one does not touch the roof, the water is not so apt to come through. My partner and I while prospecting about, used a "Compac" tent, and it answered the purpose very well.

### MISCELLANEOUS HABITATIONS

On the prairies and where no logs or other material is available, sod houses are used extensively. These are very warm when properly constructed and are easily built. Tough sod is used and is cut in squares and worked into walls. I have seen them made round and brought gradually to a point at the top which caused the roof. The sod cabin had the advantage of being warm in winter and cool in summer.

Occasionally a dug-out is used by trappers. These never suited the writer and always appeared to be damp, and only lazy trappers used them in sections where other types could be built. They were usually dug in the side of a hill and some times extended above the ground for a few feet with logs and then a roof added. When dried out, they are quite comfortable in extreme cold weather. In the extreme north, houses of snow are used. These are made of blocks and in a conical shape to form the roof. They are warm and will not melt only to a certain point even with a hot fire inside, if the temperature is very cold outside. They do melt some for a time, and are stronger and warmer after use as they gradually form into solid ice by the heat within and the cold without. Tunnels are used for entering and leaving the snow house. They are often constructed on the trail as he of the heavy woods constructs a lean-to when caught out.

The tepee is used by Indians and some Canadians. It has the advantage that a fire may be built on the ground inside, for an opening to let the smoke escape is left at the top. I never was inside of one that was not smoky, however. The covering may be anything from canvas to the skins of animals. The framework is made of poles stood conical shape and fastened at the top.

I have spent a few nights in caves that were real comfortable, but the most of these seem to be possessed with a draft that cannot be overcome. The mountainous regions often abound with great caverns and caves that may be converted into a trapper's home, but I do not advise the use of these excepting for the experience. Wild animals often make use of these caves, not only for overnight, but for hibernation and raising the young.

The houseboat is used on some of the larger streams like the Saint Lawrence and Mississippi. House-boating is a sort of romantic existence, but many hardships are attached to it. They are of no value as a trapper's habitation on streams that freeze early, and these are in the majority in the fur country.

The camp should always be located near a supply of pure water, and good fuel should be available if possible. It should never be built in low or damp places.

## CHAPTER III

### EQUIPMENT AND FOOD

#### STEEL TRAPS

TRAPS are today much nearer perfection than a few years ago. The time has passed when a trapper dropped into a local hardware store and said, "Gi'me a dozen traps." Now he knows the good and bad points of every trap made, and just what each type is intended for. He has learned from experience that any trap that will snap is not to be depended on, and that the cheapest in price is not always the cheapest in the end. One valuable animal lost by a defective or poorly constructed trap, will more than pay the difference between the price of many dozen traps, if caught by a trap that will grip and hold.

The first steel traps that were used in America were hand forged at backwoods blacksmith shops, and while crude and cumbersome, compared with the modern product, yet they were a vast improvement over the dead-fall and figure 4. In this book I am making no mention of home-made traps, for the modern trapper, working in the face of heavy competition, and out for the fur and the money, has no time to bother with comparatively useless contrivances.

The under-spring type of trap seems to be favored more by the trapper of today than other types. Traps are now made which operate by the use of a coiled spring. This kind of spring retains its expansion or tension better than others, and is made "rust proof." This spring takes up but little space and makes a compact product.

Traps are now made especially for the various species. Animals like the skunk that quickly gnaw free from the jaws of an ordinary trap are held fast by traps made especially to prevent gnawing. Double traps of the "killer" type are made to kill small animals like the muskrat.

Traps made with cast steel jaws are to be preferred to those with malleable jaws which bend easily and often fly out of place when fought by a husky animal. A long chain and a perfect working swivel should always be selected. Never use traps of a smaller size than those recommended by the maker for the particular animal you are pursuing. Sometimes a larger one is better if there is a possibility of a larger animal coming along, as in the case of a 'coon visiting a mink set, or a fox running the same trail as a skunk.

## GUNS

As question editor of different trapping publications, I am asked more about what kind of guns the prospective trapper should carry, than any other one question. There is only one type of gun worth considering for a trapline, and that is a good pistol of small calibre for shooting the trapped animals. A trapper will have little time for hunting during the trapping season, and but few sections need a heavy gun for protection. A good shot can procure enough bait with a small belt gun, and the least shooting is done in a trapping country, the better. A good rifle is sometimes needed to lay in the winter supply of meat, and there are many good reliable models in the calibres that suit the individual. A 30-30 carbine is about standard in the woods country. I do not believe in combining hunting and trapping. One who tries this will never succeed at either. It takes all the trapper's spare time searching the nooks and trails for fur sign.

### CLOTHING

The northern trapper should dress entirely in the best woolen clothing. The extreme northerner relies on the skins of animals to keep out the terrible frost king. Rabbit skin linings are about the warmest and lightest known, and are used extensively for robe lining. Sleeping-bags are also lined with the skins of rabbits. Woolen underclothes, heavy woolen outer shirt, lace leg trousers of mackinaw cloth, and two pair of heavy woolen socks, make nearly a complete outfit, and a person should always have extra changes. For footgear, I advise the pac made with leather upper and rubber bottoms for general use in the north. Soft pacs must be used with snowshoes, and rubber boots for deep water trapping. Sheepskin moccasins with the wool left on are very good for under footwear. Cowhide or moosehide pacs are good for early fall wear, but are hardly suitable for very cold or even moist weather. Buckskin suits are very good for early fall trapping and they wear like iron. These are usually made to order, as they

A HASTILY CONSTRUCTED LEAN-TO AND A PORKY FOR DINNER

are not easy procurable through the average outfitting stores.

## PACKS

Packing on the back is the usual method of getting in supplies to the far back camp as also the equipment. The pack sack is the best thing for carrying heavy loads long distances. Some sections show a preference for the pack basket, as the Adirondacks, claiming that sharp objects in a sack will hurt the back. This may be overcome by careful packing in of the objects. Fundamentally speaking, the pack sack is merely a sack made waterproof and with straps arranged for attaching to one's shoulders. A long flap should be added to completely cover the top, and which will exclude the rain or snow. Heavy waterproof canvas makes a good sack, but the fabric used in the manufacture of high grade automobile tires, is the best. The shoulder straps should be of wide leather. For a trapper that carries heavy and bulky loads, the pack should be made 28 by 3 inches. A smaller pack sack is better for traps only. Some prefer the haversack for a trapline. This is carried over one shoulder and a trap can be removed easier for setting than for the regular type of pack sack. A tump line is fitted so that it goes over the top of the head or on the forehead, and is used mainly for lifting the load from the shoulders for a few moments at a time to give them needed rest on long hauls. A trapper or other that can carry 75 pounds on his back all day is a regular he-man. Professional packers of the north have been known to carry 125 pounds all day.

## COOKING UTENSILS

The trapper's cooking utensils should be purchased with lightness of weight in view, therefore, aluminum is the best material. They should also fit one inside the other as much as possible, which method is known as "nesting" to the fraternity. A fry-pan, tea-pail, plate for each person, knife, fork, and spoon for each member of the party, cups and a few various size basins, and a stew-pan, provides all the essentials. A thermos bottle is very good where weight does not materially interfere.

## MISCELLANEOUS ARTICLES

A good knife is quite essential to the general welfare of the trapper. One large enough for preparing material for starting fires, and yet small enough to skin small fur-bearers is the kind to purchase. I do not believe in carrying a half dozen knives as some persons advise. A sheath knife is more valuable as an ornament on the trapline than for any other purpose unless it is a small one. An amateur might wish to blaze trails with a big knife, but otherwise they are not needed, for even a large animal can be easily dressed out with a good pocket knife.

A good axe and a cross-cut saw should be taken into camps in the backwoods. Steel stretchers or light, thin ones made of boards are a necessary part of an equipment. A camp light, which may be carbide, gasoline or kerosene, or even candles are used in the woods, and may be made from the fat of animals like the deer. Snowshoes are needed in the deep snow country. The coarse mesh is considered best for the trapper. One pair will seldom stand a trapper one whole season in the northland. The size should be determined by the weight of the individual using them. A toboggan is very essential if heavy loads are to be moved long distances. When drawing a loaded toboggan, if there are more than one helping, they should have an extension of rope and one go ahead of the other. This method will break a trail for the toboggan, especially if snowshoes are used.

### FOOD

Cooking has more to do with the making of good food than the materials. A good cook can take a poor piece of meat or other articles, and make it more appetizing than a poor cook could do with the best material. Take fish for instance: Some persons will tell you that perch are too bony and poor flavor to be eaten, but let a good cook prepare them by rolling alternately in the white of egg and flour, and then fry in deep fat until crisp, and I defy anyone to say that trout is better, and every bone can be eaten as with trout cooked the same way. A roast of meat should never be "basted" as is done ordinarily, but should first be seared with a red hot iron to keep in the juices, and then roasted in a hot oven. Boiled meat is much better when placed in a can without water, and then with the cover turned down lightly, placed in a kettle full of water and cooked in that way until completed. Even the art of making tea is not known by the majority. Tea should be placed in cold water and is ready to serve when it arrives at the boiling point. Coffee is never improved by boiling. I will now give a few recipes that I have tried out in the woods and found satisfactory.

### SOUR DOUGH SPONGE

To one quart of warm water, add one cup sugar, and flour to make a heavy batter. Set in a warm place until it ferments, which can be told by the bubbles arising to the top. For bread, add two teaspoonfuls of salt, two of bacon grease or butter, and flour to make a stiff dough. Knead six minutes, and set in a warm place to rise, then knead again and cut into loaves and put in pans. When it rises again, bake in medium oven. For flop cakes, take one pint of batter and add one teaspoon salt, one quart flour and water or milk to make the proper consistency. Add one-half teaspoon soda and fry quickly.

### FRIED BISCUITS

Mix one egg or its equivalent in egg powder with one teaspoon of soda. Add two tablespoonfuls bacon grease, one teaspoon sugar, and flour to make a thick batter. Fry in hot grease.

### DUMPLINGS

These are sometimes called dough gods in the woods. Cook meat until tender. Season with salt and pepper. Add sliced potatoes. Take a pint of flour and mix with one teaspoonful of cream of tartar and one spoonful of soda. A pinch of salt, and a little butter or bacon grease. Then add water or preferably milk until the batter will hold its shape when dropped from a spoon. Then place on top of the potatoes and meat, and cover to hold the steam and boil.

#### MEAL FLAP JACKS

Scald two cups of meal with a pint of boiling water, beating to a smooth mash; thin with one quart of sour milk, in which is dissolved one teaspoon of soda. Add salt and egg powder or two eggs, and enough flour to form suitable pancake batter. Fry on hot griddle.

#### LIST OF FOOD FOR ONE PERSON TWO WEEKS

This may be varied according to the taste of the individual.

| | | | |
|---|---|---|---|
| White flour | 10 lbs. | Coffee | ½ lb. |
| Bacon | 8 lbs. | Tea | ¼ lb. |
| Sugar | 10 lbs. | Baking powder | ¼ lb. |
| Whole peas | 1 lb. | Soda | ¼ lb. |
| Beans | 2 lbs. | Corn meal | 5 lbs. |
| Egg powder | 1 lb. | Chocolate | 1 lb. |
| Dried vegetables | 3 lbs. | Raisins | 1 lb. |
| Salt | ½ lb. | Rice | 1 lb. |
| Pepper | 2 oz. | | |

A person when going into the woods should never depend too much on getting their food on the way. An expert woodsman can help out his food supply from nature's commissary department, such as fish, wild game, berries, roots, etc. The tyro will not always be able to procure food in this manner.

Another thing to be remembered is that one will eat nearly double his usual amount when roaming about in the woods and fields or following a long trapline.

Never try to live on meats alone or any other one food, for the human body needs certain elements which are only found in the different foods, and a person must be at his best to tend a trapline.

## CHAPTER IV

### THINGS EVERY TRAPPER SHOULD KNOW
#### INJURIES—FIRST AID

BEFORE going into the far back woods for a winter's trapping, a person should familiarize himself with all the best first aid methods, and make sure that his partner does likewise.

To stop blood from flowing, apply pressure directly over the wound or by means of a compress. To make a tourniquet, tie a handkerchief or bandage between the wound and the heart, place a pebble if possible, over the blood vessel and twist by inserting a stick.

Broken bones must be kept in place by splints made of thin pieces of wood. They should be padded with cloth.

For snake bite, use a tourniquet between the bite and the heart, loosening occasionally. Cut the wound so it will bleed freely. Sear with a hot iron.

For apparent drowning, remove water from the mouth. Draw the tongue forward. Kneel at the patient's side, and draw the arms upward and backward until the patient's hands touch the ground behind his head. Hold three seconds, and carry downward slowly, pressing firmly on the chest. Keep this up for at least one hour.

For burns exclude air and treat with a solution of baking soda and water. Where blisters are formed, let out the water by pricking with a needle that has been previously passed through a flame. When clothing sticks to the flesh, never forcibly remove it, but cut close to the wounds and soak in oil until they free easily.

Careful trappers go to their physician and get common remedies before leaving for the wilderness. These must be properly labeled and the dosage properly marked. I remember the first winter that my partner and I spent in the wilds. We took an elaborate medicinal equipment with us and the correct dose was marked on each vial, but unfortunately we neglected learning what any of the remedies were for. Good luck was with us, however, and neither one was sick. One night an old guide stumbled into our cabin in a sick condition, vowing that he was going to pass out of the picture, so to speak. We reassured him that he had a good chance to kill many deer before his time came, for were we not prepared for just such emergency as this. There was just one thing to be done and we did it. We gave him a dose or two from every vial in the case, and you can believe it or not, that bird went on his way rejoicing on the following morning.

A small vial of iodine, a few rolls of bandaging, a curved needle for sewing flesh, and some silk thread are quite essential in the outfit of a woodsman. Even if your own party does not need any of the before-mentioned articles, one can sometimes save a life where a doctor cannot be reached quickly.

### FIRE PREVENTION AND FIGHTING

Nothing ruins a good trapping region like a forest fire, which not only kills many of the woods' inhabitants, but ruins the natural cover and dens of both fur-bearers and game.

Never be careless with fire, for it is a fine servant but a poor master. Do not throw a match away until you are sure it is cold. Cigarette stubs hold fire for many minutes and have been the direct cause of the devastation of thousands of acres of forest. Scrape away the leaves before building a campfire, and do not make a larger one than is needed. It is much easier to warm one's self by building a small fire and getting close to it, than by making a large one and being obliged to get far back. When leaving camp, do not guess that the fire is out, but be positive.

If you find a fire, try and put it out; it is evidently easier done at that time than it would be later. The usual method is to cut a trail all around it, removing all inflammable material from this space. Experienced fire fighters sometimes start another fire, making sure that it burns in the direction of the original fire. When the two fires meet they must go out.

### COLLECTING THE MEAT SUPPLY

This book was written for trappers, but I will mention a few words on hunting, knowing that the average trapper exists to a great extent on game.

Probably the commonest game and the animal most used for food is the deer. They winter in the foothills, ranging higher as the snow melts. In summer, they feed on grass in the open places, and later are found eating the tender shoots from the raspberry, hazel and others, and when the beechnuts fall, they are quite sure to be on the beech ridges.

THE TYPE OF TRAPPER WHO TRAPS ALL SEASON, BUT NEVER BUYS ANY TRAPS

Deer and other animals of the wilds are keen-scented and the hunter should work against the wind or breeze. Only the most silent trailers can follow a deer track close enough to the animal to get in a killing shot without scaring the animal. Do not hunt any game by rushing through the woods. The best hunters go slowly and noiselessly. Sit down and be silent when in a good section.

When a kill is made, hang the animal up by the hind legs, slit the skin through the middle of the breast and continue to the root of the tail, and then along each leg to the joint. Remove the legs at the joint. Cut through the abdomen and make an incision the entire length of the body, using a hatchet or heavy hunting knife to cut the breast bone. Be careful not to cut the intestines. Then remove the entire contents. The liver and heart are usually reserved for food.

To "jerk" venison or other meat, use lean cuts made into long thin strips, and lay them on a frame of green wooden strips about one yard from the ground. Then build a small, smoky fire underneath and keep it burning until the meat is absolutely dry.

The flesh of rabbits, 'coon, 'possum, beaver, bear, muskrat, and porcupine are all used for food by trappers.

### GETTING LOST

The main thing that keeps many inexperienced trappers out of the big woods, is the fear of getting lost. There is little danger in this if the person is of average intelligence and does not lose his head. A good compass should be carried and one should know which end of the needle points north.

Streams usually run in the same general direction in every territory and one can keep his direction by following these. The only exception is along divides in the mountain regions.

Blazed trails are made by clipping a piece of bark as large as a man's hand from trees that are in line and show plainly. The blaze marks must be made on both sides of the trees or the trail can only be followed one way. Few trappers care to trap over a "blazed trail," for any person could follow it and locate the sets.

In the mountain regions, the passes and notches should be used when going from one section to another, for it is often impossible to go directly over a range, and one who tried it might end up in a chasm with a broken neck.

Should a person discover that he has lost his way, it is best to sit down and reason the thing out. Never wander aimlessly about or rush on, hoping to come to some place you will recognize. If it is near night, erect shelter and prepare to await the morning's light. Then in the morning, decide on a course and follow it. If the sun is shining, this will guide you, otherwise use your compass. If you have neither one to guide you, remember that the trees generally lean towards the south with their tips, and heavier bark grows on the north side. When you come to a stream, follow it in the direction the water is flowing.

### SELECTING A PARTNER

This applies to partners for the season only and not life partners, for a nomadic partner like myself could hardly advise how to pick a "peach," among the great garden of lemons.

A trapper is much better off without a partner than with a poor one. By this statement, I do not mean a person who is new at the game, for we all had to learn, and I have spent some pleasant periods with amateur trappers who were willing to work and learn. If there is any meanness in a person, and I assume that we all are endowed with a certain amount of this doubtful quality, it will show up when two persons have suffered or enjoyed each other's society for six months in the backwoods where no other voice has been heard. Petty arguments at this time assume large proportions, and blood has been spilled for a mere nothing.

A seasoned partner is surer to stay by one the winter through, and others should be tried out before the open season. Do not unjustly accuse your partner if he fails to bring in as many furs as yourself. He may have a poorer line or lack the experience. Rather go around with him a day, and try to set him right.

A dog makes a fine partner when none other suitable one is available. They should, however, be left in camp when one is putting out traps, but at other times they often locate animal dens that a person could never ferret out. The breed of dog must be chosen by the owner. Different localities use the various species. The husky is used in the northland for transporting the trapper to and from his grounds and carrying in food and equipment. The "husky" is a mixture of breeds.

## OUTDOOR PHOTOGRAPHY

Often there are scenes along the trapline that one would give much in after years to see once more. Then it is possible that good photographs of animals in their natural state, may be sold for good money. For these purposes the trapper and outdoorsman should carry a camera. The trapper's camera should be light and compact, yet efficient and practical, and possess a good lens. Wild animal photographs and trapline scenes are usually made under difficult conditions of light. This is the reason we see such a large percentage of dull, dark photographs among the outdoor fraternity.

Animals and fur-bearers are particularly hard to photograph, for being quick of movement, a short exposure must be given, and with poor light of the woods this is impossible—unless the person is equipped with a lens working sharply at a large aperture. An anastigmat lens working at F:4-5 is about right for the kind of work mentioned, and the shutter should be equally good. The light should not be directly in front of the camera, and an exposure of 1-10th of a second will be fast enough to avoid blurring by movement under ordinary conditions. This would be for light shade with the lens just mentioned at wide open. Speed is lost when the shutter is stopped down, but the image will be sharper.

Do not hurry about photograph making. Correct composition has much to do with a good photograph. Natural poses in animals are the only kind that are valuable. Keep the film in a dry place both before and after exposing.

## CHAPTER V

### ADIRONDACK TRAPPING

"Where the red deer leaps and the panther creeps,
Where the trout leaps high at the hovering fly,
And the eagle's cry bodes a tempest nigh,
This is my home—in the mountains alone."

AFTER traveling many thousands of miles in search of ideal trapping grounds, I find that there is no place that offers more diversion than the 'Dacks. In the foothills one finds skunk, fox, 'coon, weasel, and mink, while the silences farther back harbor fisher, marten, 'cats, and otter, as well as some of the others. There are 500,000 acres in the Adirondacks, and practically all of this has a natural cover of giant forest trees, or thick brush and second growth. Almost one-half of the entire area consists of ponds, lakes, and streams. Surely this is a natural haunt for the things of the wild.

The State of New York is the largest land owner in the Adirondacks. This property has been set aside for the use of citizens, and no lumbering is done. Some of the land was purchased from lumber companies who had taken the most of the green timber. Since then a new growth has sprung up, and today there are great tracts where one can travel for days and seldom see open sky.

SEARCHING FOR MINK SIGNS IN THE DEEP FOREST IN MID-WINTER

The state has erected many camps in beautiful spots, but these are to be used by a transient people only. Trappers are not allowed to build permanent camps on state land, but they may use tents and trap where they wish, providing they have a license for the purpose.

The Adirondack region is easily accessible, yet there are some of the remotest mountain fastnesses in America to be found there. The scenery is truly wonderful, and is less barren and more forest covered than many other wilderness sections. Trappers however, cannot exist on beautiful scenes, but are more interested in the fur-bearers that make their home there. In one day's travel when there was a tracking snow, I saw the trails of three otter, one fisher, two marten, a dozen mink, and dozens of foxes. This was of course a good day and in a good section.

The professional Adirondack trapper often has a line of traps out that extends fifty miles. This distance is covered in two or three days, depending on the traveling. This necessitates a headquarters camp or one or more overnight camps. The temperature goes very low at intervals during the winter, and it is not unusual for 50 degrees below zero to remain for a week. Being well sheltered, there is no wind excepting on the mountain tops, and the natives, provided as they are with an abundance of hardwood, rarely suffer from cold.

Snow arrives about November first and lasts until late April. In deeply sheltered spots and on the highest summits, there is snow nearly the year round. This snow and cold causes the fur-bearers to grow a thick coat of fur, and continuous traveling in the shadows of the forest, does not tend to fade it out like fur-bearers of the open that move about in daytime, and many species of the Adirondack fur-bearers have pelts that command more money than others of the same State.

Few common animals like the muskrat are found far back in the wooded sections. Regarding the 'rat, this is not because the animal does not like seclusion, but because the icy water of the mountain streams and ponds are not adapted to growing the plants which constitute the natural food of the 'rat. Occasionally one of these little fur-bearers will be taken however, but unlike the balance of the Adirondack denizens, the fur is of a poor quality the skin light and papery.

The mainstay of the Adirondack trappers are mink and fox. Blind trapping is used by the most expert for both of these animals. A few of the best trappers average two foxes each day during the best of the season. The State does not protect the fox by law, and many trappers begin operating in early October. Animals taken at this time are put into pens to await the priming of their fur, or sold to fur farmers as stock. Otter are also not protected, but these glossy fur-bearers are not easy to keep in a pen, and often die of apparent longing for the long trails amid the wilds.

The canoe and guide-boat which is a kind of cross between a canoe and a skiff, are used whenever possible for taking supplies into camp. Well connected waterways enable one to go to almost every part. Where boats cannot be used, one must

A GOOD MINK AND OTTER STREAM IN THE ADIRONDACKS

pack in his outfit on his back, or wait for snow, when the toboggan may be used. The pack basket is preferred to the sack in the Adirondack region. These baskets are made of strips of ash or other wood, and most native Adirondackers know how to construct their own.

Considering the amount of hunters that annually visit the Adirondack forest, game is fairly plentiful. This is due mainly to the fact that the cover is good and affords the best protection to the haunters of the woods. Deer are the largest animals sought, unless it is the bear, but occasionally an odd moose or elk is reported seen. The deer are hunted mainly by the method known as "driving." The natives know the deer trails, and placing hunters on these natural runs, they circle about and by barking like dogs and making other noise, scare the animals until they run close enough to the watchers for a successful shot. The law allows one to keep the meat after the closed season if a permit is secured, and many trappers have their meat stored up for the season. Only one deer is allowed to a hunter, but a large one will furnish meat for a long time.

Grouse are plentiful and furnish fine sport and food. In the most secluded places they are hardly wild enough to make interesting hunting, until shot at a few times, when they become more wary. Dogs are not permitted to roam the forest unless tagged for that purpose.

The natives of the 'Dacks are a very hospitable people, and no stranger goes hungry or without shelter. Many old timers live nomadic existences

A TRAPPER'S CABIN WITH MOUNTAINOUS SURROUNDINGS

in snug log cabins dozens of miles from civilization. They make two or three trips to the nearest village for supplies each year. They have no desire to leave their homes, and invariably their last request is to be buried close to their cabins where they spent their life. These old timers are all trappers, and can relate wonderful stories if they can be induced to do so.

Stories of Indian fights and encounters with wild animals that are more entrancing than any fiction are often told. They tell of days when the carcass of a deer would not remain on the back of the camp one night, before some great prowler would remove it.

The trapper can always be assured of a variety of fish in the Adirondacks, and a sizzling dish of these are always a welcome addition to a trapper's table. Brook trout, lake trout, northern pike, pickerel, and bass are among the leaders—each a stirring call to the angler.

Legend says that the first settler in the Adirondacks was an Indian by the name of Benedict Sabael, who left the Province of Quebec in the early seventies. It is possible that other Indians had made this their hunting ground much earlier. Reuben Rist was the first white settler in the Adirondacks proper, who built his home on the shore of Indian Lake. He was supposed to have been killed by Indians at a later date.

During all of our early wars, much fighting was done in or adjacent to the Adirondacks. During 1600, the French came down from Quebec to attack the Iroquois who were stationed in the foothills.

They became hopelessly lost, and many were killed by the Indians.

During the French and Indian wars, battles were fought at Fort William Henry at Lake George, and the vicinity of Ticonderoga witnessed bloody fighting. This fort was taken from the British during the Revolution by Ethan Allen and his Green Mountain Boys.

Dozens of engagements were fought to the bitter end along the foothills. The invaders came down from the north in boats by way of Lake Champlain, named for its discoverer. The Iroquois were the most powerful Indian tribe.

It will pay any reader to make a trip to the Adirondacks, whether he be interested in trapping or not. Good auto roads cross much of this land of beauty and a kaleidoscope panorama of wonderful visions are constantly unfolding. Nature is never more sublime.

## CHAPTER VI

### THE AUTO TRAPLINE

"SPOT trapping" with an automobile has become one of the greatest branches of our trapping industry. I know of no particular kind of trapping that offers better opportunities or greater remuneration than that mentioned at the beginning of this chapter. Almost any part of America has some kind of "spot trapping," and with reliable machines offered at today's prices, no trapper can afford to be without one.

Contrary to the general belief, the auto trapper does less to exterminate the species than any other trapper. If he has any sense of fairness in him, he will leave a section the moment the animals get scarce, and with a good car ready, it is very easy to go where trapping is better and leave the balance for seed. Trappers who have no way of moving about often trap a section until no breeders are left, thus ruining their chance of a continuous occupation.

There are many cars adapted to auto trapping. Many auto manufacturers now build models with a thought of camping in view. A study of the various catalogs will prove this. Some of the bodies are veritable homes on wheels. A trapper in a comparatively level section can use one of these or build just what he needs and place it on a chassis, but he of the mountain roads will stick to the regular type and either stay in camps constructed for that purpose or occupy tents. There are many of the latter on the market, from the palatial apartment tent, to the piece of canvas known to trappers as a "tarp."

To trappers who move very often, I suggest the wedge style tent. This is easily and quickly set up, and is warmer than most other types. For a single "spot trapper," the 5x7 foot size will suffice as sleeping quarters, but where there are two or more, or where trappers set up near streams or other good trapping ground for a week at a time, I would prefer a 10x12 tent with a 4-foot wall. A stove should be provided for heat and for cooking, and it should be large enough so that a fire would keep all night. I once used a small coal stove when adjacent to sections where I could procure this fuel easily, and I never spent as comfortable a time in a tent.

An auto can be used in many other ways to further the interests of a trapper, it will haul loads of food and equipment close to camps of the all-winter variety, and may be used to a great advantage in prospecting for fur.

The auto trapper can handle more traps than any other type, especially if he covers various kinds of territory and traps for the different animals in each section. Weight is of no great consideration to a trapper equipped with a good car, and he can take a few extra traps along. 500 traps are none too many for an energetic "spot trapper" with a car. Of course there are sections on the plains where one would be trapping for coyotes and badgers where this would be more than one could use, but in a good muskrat section, they can be placed thickly and then in a few days move to new localities.

A "SPOT TRAPPER"

No kind of trapping offers such diversion as "auto trapping." Leaving the Saint Lawrence Valley at early morning, I have worked a good 'rat section, then skunk, 'coon and fox, beaver and otter, and ended up at night in a fisher and marten region. But it takes a lot of study to learn the habits of so many different kinds of animals.

A folding cot will suffice as a bed for the auto trapper, as he will have little time or inclination to make bough beds. Three or more woolen blankets should be carried at all times by the trapper of the northland.

Occasionally a used car may be purchased cheaply and will give good satisfaction. No one should contemplate purchasing a second hand car, however, without having some person along that understands natural wear and conditions of a car. Compression can be tested by grasping the crank and turning each piston up quickly. If a cylinder is weaker than the rest, there is something wrong. This may be the result of faulty valves, worn cylinders, weak rings, or scored cylinders. Some of these faults are easily remedied while others are costly. Wear can sometimes be determined by putting the car in gear and turning on the crank. If the crank turns far before the car starts to move, there is much wear in the gears, universal joint, and in other places. The trapper's car gets very hard use and should be in first class condition, for a break in the trapping season would mean more than the price of a new car.

The cost of an outfit for auto trapping will vary so much in the different localities that no universal price could be named. Then it depends on weather conditions. An outfit that would be fine for a trapper of Southern United States, along the 'rat and 'coon marshes, would never suffice for the bleak, cold regions of the northland, bucking snowbanks with the car, and camping in zero weather.

Besides being the most profitable branch of trapping, I get as much enjoyment from the "auto trapline" as any type of trapping. Having worked the same sections with my car for a considerable number of seasons, I have learned the best pockets. the natural camp-sites, and the best animal runs. Muskrat ponds, streams, and marshes have netted me the greatest amounts of money for the labor involved, but spot trapping for foxes along the Adirondack foothills has turned me many an honest dollar. A spot trapper with a good car in a favorable section should pick up $50 worth of fur each day during the best of the season. But he would have to be an experienced trapper, and know the habits of the citizens of the wild.

One reason that a trapper can get more enjoyment from auto trapping than some other forms, is that many necessities and even luxuries can be carried that could not be tolerated on a wilderness trapline. I've camped out in the far back places in open (Siwash) camps and nearly froze, because I could not pack in needed equipment for comfort, but a person who does this is only laying a foundation for a weakened old age and much suffering. And I've slept in a snug stove heated tent, on a spring cot, with a mattress and plenty of blankets and pillows, and realized that life was worth the living on an "auto trapline."

## CHAPTER VII

## THE FOX

"Fool the animal's nose and you have him fooled entirely."—DAILEY.

### HAUNTS AND HABITS

THE fox, red renegade of the trails, is one of the slyest fur-bearers in America. With every man's hand against him, and with little protection from the game laws, this animal is holding his own in numbers and is found in more or less plentiful numbers in almost every part of the United States and Canada. The fox is of the dog family, and exists in various colors from the common red, to blacks, silver-grays, blue, white, plain gray, and mixed. The most valuable is the silver-black variety, and the least valuable the woods gray.

The fox shows little preference for any particular kind of territory, wilderness, or settlement, mountain or plain. If there are natural fox foods the animal will be found there. The blacks, silvers, and some of the others are rarely found other than in the extreme northland, while the gray is of the sunny South.

It is commonly believed that foxes of the far back wilderness are easier to take in game traps than near the farmlands. The fact is that it is just the opposite, for during their wanderings in proximity to mankind, they become accustomed to human odor and learn to fear it less. Only when coupled with unusual circumstances does the fox show fear of this odor. For instance: If a farmer walks over a cow trail in search of his cattle, the animal will pass over this same trail immediately afterward, or if a ploughman makes a fresh furrow, a fox is apt to run this within twenty-four hours. If either one stops and makes peculiar marks, or piles something in the trail, the approaching fox is alert, and will usually shy off and go around this. Therefore, a trapper should act as natural as possible when pursuing this animal, or in fact any others of the elusive species.

Not only does the fox depend on his own existence by his natural cunning, but he gains his food in the same manner. Stealthiness of approach is another of his natural talents. He is also very fleet of foot, and almost tireless on the trail. Nocturnal in his habits, yet he often wanders about in the partly sheltered spots during daytime.

The natural food of the fox is flesh, and small animals and birds are his prey. Foxes in captivity will eat vegetables, grains, fruit, and drink milk. They appear quite fond of fish. Rabbits being more plentiful than other prey, the fox depends on these for the bulk of his food. I have noted the tracks in fresh snow where a fox crept upon a feeding rabbit. Always he took advantage of every tree, hummock, or other object that kept him sheltered from the sight of his victim. The fox always hunts with the wind in his favor. When within six feet of the unsuspecting rabbit, he made a spring, and a few bits of fur and spatters of crimson on the snow, told the balance of the story.

A FOX SET IN ANIMAL TRAIL, TRAP UNCOVERED

However, the fox makes mistakes, and I had the opportunity of watching one err in his judgment. I was prospecting for fur in the Adirondack region, and was following the shoreline of a pond in search of otter sign. It was rather a marshy pond and considerable reeds grew along the shore. Suddenly I noted a pair of whistler ducks working among the reeds, apparently looking for frogs or tiny fishes. I was about to pot one of them with a gun I carried, when some rods back I saw a slight movement. In a moment I could discern the outline of a fox cautiously approaching the feeding ducks. So absorbed was it in gaining a feed of these juicy morsels, that he failed to notice me, although the wind was in my favor, and I hid back of a stump. Step by step the animal moved in the direction of the wild ducks, and while a wild duck is one of the hardest creatures of the outdoors to approach, they did not see him. When within a short distance I could see the form of the fox tense, and the usually flowing tail stuck straight out. Then his body shot into space, but at that moment, some instinct warned the ducks, and they arose with a loud quacking. A lone feather drifted back, proving that the fox reckoned closely. Never did I witness a more bitter look of chagrin, than that depicted on the features and in the attitude of that fox. I could have shot him easily, but the fur was not yet prime, and I passed him up, to make some poor nomad of the trapline happy or otherwise.

The fox dens in various places, but always with the thought of security in view. Under great rocky ledges is the favorite location, but in a sand country they dig dens to such an extensive depth that it is about impossible to remove one. Only during the mating season and while raising the young, or when hard pursued, do they make use of regular dens. At other times they hide in hollow logs, stumps, or leaning trees, or in impenetrable thickets.

Foxes are hunted with dogs to an even greater extent than they are trapped. A good fox-hound is one that will run no other animal. He must be a sure trailer, a good barker, and a stayer. Such dogs often bring one hundred dollars or more. The fox will continually try to elude the pursuing hounds.

One of his favorite tricks is to climb on a fence, walk the top of it for a few rods and then jump to an adjacent rock and continue to keep on other objects than the ground. He will back track and jump sideways, and occasionally when hard pressed will take to water for a short distance.

The raising of black and silver foxes has gained popularity faster than any industry I have ever known. All over the Northland these farms can be found. Very little fur has yet been marketed by these farms as demand for stock to start or increase other farms has handled all the surplus. Only the culls have found their way to the fur market. The ranch raised foxes, like the wild, have but one litter each year. At least this is the rule. The female will not mate with every male that is placed in her pen but may reject a half dozen before one is selected that suits, but once they are mated they remember each other for life.

ADIRONDACK FOOTHILL SCENERY. GOOD FOX COUNTRY

There is no doubt in my mind that a fox can reason to a certain extent, but unlike the human, they cannot think of two things at once. Therefore, always try to attract the atention of the animal from your trap at each set. I have known experts to tie a bright string to a tree near the set for this purpose. The whole dog family is also curious at all times regarding the unusual. I read of an old wolf that had fooled every trapper for years to fall for a trap placed by the side of a jug with the cork out, and which made a weird whistling noise when the wind blew. But I am not advocating the "jug set."

Certain persons have a power over animals that makes it easy for them to trap the elusive species. Did you ever notice that individuals existed that a dog would always bite at any opportunity, and that others could be friends with any dog? Wild animals apparently fear the odor of certain persons more than others. The deeper science of the thing seems to be that an animal can distinguish whether the individual is intending harm or not by his odor alone. Surely such emotions as anger shows plainly on the face. Why not in the odor when sniffed by a nose much better developed than that possessed by humans? But I do not believe any animal gets any reasonable power through the sense of sight. A hound never recognizes his master until he gets a sniff or two. An animal certainly can detect odor a long distance. I have witnessed a fox-hound riding in an automobile which would suddenly try to scramble out, and when allowed to do so, would go directly to a track ten rods or more away. This sense of smell however, is more highly developed in some animals of the same species than in others. This accounts for the fact that occasionally a fox will fall for an ordinary uncovered skunk trap. After making a few such catches, some trappers say that a fox is easy caught and that odor does not have to be eliminated. This is not the rule, and the best fox trapper I ever knew, waded along the shores of streams and made his sets within reach of the water. He then splashed water over the set.

A good way to learn the habits of the fox or any other fur-bearer is to follow one's tracks after a good tracking snow. Learning animal habits is the first lesson in the school of trapping. Without this knowledge, no person can ever succeed in the gentle art of trapping.

Some nature fakirs tell of instances where foxes turned traps bottom side up, and even poked sticks in them. There is nothing to this. Such happenings are usually the result of some joker or trapping competitor who wished to put the set out of order.

### TRAPPING METHODS

It is a common belief that the successful trappers of foxes and other sly fur-bearers have a wonderful, secret scent that draws the animals to the trap, and holds them until caught. Trappers who did not care to divulge the real secrets, often evaded mention of facts, by implying that their scents did the trick. The fact is that no scent ever improved a poorly made set. Scents however, may aid in taking a fox at a properly made set. The

A FOX THAT WAS NOT SLY ENOUGH

amateur had better not mix with scents until he can catch foxes without them. Plenty of good sets have been ruined by the improper use of artificial scent.

Scents, however, may be used successfully in connection with properly made sets. The best drawing scent in the world is the odor of natural food. Strong odors are created by rotting cat-flesh, and adding skunk essence, horse's hoof parings, beaver castor, musk, fish-oil, anise oil, rotted mice, and any other terrible odors. There is no general rule for mixing this dope up. The flesh of the cats and other things is cut into small pieces and placed in jars early in the fall. The fish oil that is used in scent making is procured by rotting small fish in water and then skimming the oil from the top.

The trapper that uses scents should keep changing the odors as the foxes in his vicinity will soon associate a regularly used odor with danger and traps. Only small quantities of scent should ever be used at one time, and this ought to be placed on a stick or some object near the set.

The most successful fox set in America is the water hole set. This varies some with different trappers and in different sections, but the principle is the same. Spring water is used in the North for the reason that it does not freeze easily, and once the set is made, it need not be molested until a catch is made. I know of no other fox set that does not get out of condition readily. In making this set, one should locate the water close by a section where foxes are known to dwell or pass. Flesh bait should be placed on the top of a stick so that it appears to be floating on top of the water.

and should be about four feet from the shore or land. Then flat stones should be placed one on top of the other until they come within two inches of the top of the water, about half way between the bait and land. Then the trap should be placed on the stone and moss worked in around it until the whole appears like a moss covered stone. Some trappers pack moss under the trap pan so that it will not work easily. They do this for the reason that the fox will reach out and tap the moss easily before stepping on it.

Trail or blind sets are used more than any other and will take foxes easily if odor is eliminated before the fox arrives.

Before making a blind set, the trap should be boiled in pure water, or allowed to lay in a running stream for at least one week. Boiling in various barks and boughs only adds to the foreign odors. Traps should be covered with material from local surroundings which will harmonize with the natural odors of the section where the set is made. For instance: pine needles would never do in a cedar country, but the dead leaves of the cedar should be used instead. The fluff from cat-tails is used extensively in the lowlands. Dry sand in the sand country. Sand, however, freezes easily. This can be remedied by baking the sand until there is absolutely no moisture in it, and even then a rain will wet it up. Anywhere that foxes run regularly will suffice for a trail set. Old cow or deer trails, plowed furrows, along rocky bluffs, animal trails leading to a carcass of a larger animal, along streams, around old hay and straw stacks, are all good locations to make blind sets. When making a trail set, select the narrowest spot and make an excavation so that the trap will be level or flush with the ground. Then line this hole with dry material and place in the trap. Clean gloves should be worn, and rubber footwear leaves the least odor. I have known trappers to stand on a piece of bark when making a set. During a snow or rainstorm is a good time to make sets for elusive animals, for the storms automatically eradicate odors. I advise that traps set for foxes should be fastened with a pronged drag. Occasionally there is a natural object close by the set that may be used, but it should be movable. A fox is easily held in a trap, but a powerful trap must be used so that it will work through thick coverings. The number 2 trap has always been considered the fox trap, but some of the best trappers use the 3 or 3XK.

An old log that lies across a stream makes an excellent location for a blind set. A very small stick can be placed in an upright position under the trap pan to prevent smaller animals from springing the trap. The pin holding the pan may be made tighter by riveting with a hammer. This makes the pan work harder.

Canadian trappers depend on the snare to capture foxes, at least some of them do. They kill an old horse, cow, or some other large animal in a good fox section, and cover it with brush. After the animals get to feeding and have learned to crawl through the brush, the trapper places his snares in the most likely places. The Canadian farmland trapper gets many a fox with the manure-pile set. He draws out loads of horse manure and puts it in piles. Sometimes he throws a beefhead or other

THE AUTHOR WITH A TRAPPED FOX

bait on top of the pile. When he wishes to set the traps, he drives close to the pile and sets the trap from the sleigh. The ammonia in horse-manure kills the trap odors. Even if no bait is placed on the pile, foxes will work about it in search of mice. A mound of any kind is a good location for a set. A muskrat or beaver house is no exception.

Bait sets are used when there are no natural places for blind or trail sets. The baits should be put out early and be replaced as the animals eat them up. During a light snow is the best time to put in the trap. Of course one never knows to what extent a snowfall may be, but even ten inches of light snow will not materially interfere with a smooth-working trap.

A large bait is better than a small one for the reason that the natural odors will not freeze out so easily. Years ago when big game was very plentiful and game laws few, trappers used to go about through the woods in the early fall and shoot down animals, knowing that by the time fur was prime, many fur-bearers including fox, would be feeding from them. There are far back places where this practice is carried on at the present time, but this method is never to be commended.

In sections where many deer, moose, elk, etc., are killed by hunters each fall, are good places to trap fox, for the entrails and waste parts of the animals are invariably left where the killing was made, which coaxes all kinds of fur-bearers out to feed. Where such baits are not available, one can usually purchase wornout horses at the price of the hide, and horse-flesh is excellent fox bait. Adjacent to great lumbering operations, many horses are killed in accidents each season, and a fox will go nearly anywhere where there is natural food. I've known them to smell about my venison that was hung at the back of the cabin while I slept.

Deep snow trapping for fox is considered the most difficult, and at this time, few other fur-bearers are moving, therefore the professional fox trapper must be able to take them at this time as well as any other. Out in the farmlands, the snow usually drifts every day and is constantly changing in its formation. The farmland fox trapper at this time must seek the sheltered spots to make his sets. Under dense pine or spruce trees are suitable spots, but the bait ought to be thrown in during the fall. A skunk carcass is the best bait at this time, for it is the only thing that will hold its odor. The carcass of a house cat is also good. These should be thrown carelessly down as if dropped by a trapper, for the fox learn that many bits of food is obtainable by following the trapper of smaller fur-bearers.

The backwoods fox trapper will not be bothered materially by drifting snow in mid-winter, but heavy snow-falls will cover his sets too deeply. At this time I have a set which has picked off many sly reds, and it will work for wolves, lynx, or any other rabbit hunting fur-bearers. In the swamp sections are always deep rabbit trails and every trapper is aware that foxes follow these trails. He will also know that a trap set in such trail would catch a rabbit every minute during the night. Now in every swamp there are many fallen trees and logs. The rabbit will always jump completely over these obstructions, but the fox will jump on top of the log, and then leap as far as possible. The secret is out: Conceal your trap carefully on top of the log. A balsam bough or other brush is used to cover a fox trap with snow, leaving less odor than the hands and doing the work much better. Some trappers place tissue paper over their fox traps before any other covering. Others make bags of tissue paper and paraffine them to keep out dampness. The fox, however, will recognize the strange odor of paraffine. Natural coverings of material like pine needles in a pine country is better in the estimation of the writer. Fluff from cat-tails or pure wool is sometimes placed under the trap pan to keep heavier material from preventing the functioning of the trap.

After the deep snows come, the foxes will often follow the streams where it is easier traveling. Often one can locate where the animal has left uneaten food in these places and a trap covered nearby has a chance to make a catch. Around old abandoned camps and sawmills are likely places to look for fox signs. I caught a nice bunch of foxes once on a pile of sawdust, and I used no bait of any kind, just made a purely blind set in the dust.

In sections where cotton-tail rabbits are plentiful, one can often take foxes around their den entrances. These rabbits live in wood-chuck burrows and in hollow logs. The fox trap should be slightly to one side of the rabbit run, for the fox will work all around the den. One may occasionally catch a rabbit in these sets, and often a fox will eat the victim while it is yet in the trap. Once I had a small rabbit in a fox set and the fox arrived while the rabbit was struggling to get free. There was a fresh tracking snow and I could see where the fox had spent the entire night circling about, obviously afraid to take the food before him. I killed the catch and left it in the trap and concealed three traps nearby and got the fox the following night.

One must have plenty of perseverance in trapping foxes. The amateur often gives up just when he should be commencing. After the first fox is caught, the new beginner feels like a great trapper and prepares to take them by the dozens. It takes a lifetime of trapping to learn all there is about taking this animal.

There are more fox specialists than any other type or kind of trapping. Here in the Adirondack Mountains there are trappers who kick greatly if any other fur-bearer gets in their sets. Trappers of this type set out as many as two hundred fox traps. Some of the best take nearly one hundred foxes in a season, but the majority catch much less.

Foxes should be skinned "cased," and are usually stretched with the fur out, the hide being so thin that it will dry in this manner.

The grading is done on a basis of quality even more than size, as the fur varies much in the same localities. Silkiness of the fur is much to be desired. The fur is used mainly for ladies' scarf making and in trimming various clothes of the fair sex. Being very light in weight, it is used much for the so-called summer furs. The prices of the average northern fox skin runs from $200 for a choice silver to $1.00 for a wood's gray, being the greatest range of prices of any animal of the fur-bearing species.

## CHAPTER VIII

## THE SKUNK AND HOW TO TRAP IT

### HABITS AND HAUNTS

TO be called a "Skunk" is usually considered a base insult, but to find one of these "woods kitties" in your trap on a cold November morning, is a pleasure indeed, especially if it happens to be of the darker varieties.

Few fur-bearers are better known or scattered over a wider territory than the skunk, known in some sections of the United States, particularly in the southern part as a "pole-cat." The little civet is of the same family, and what is said in this chapter regarding skunks will also apply where this animal is concerned.

The skunk is not a habitat of the great wilderness sections excepting in a minus quantity. Rather, it makes its home in proximity to mankind, apparently realizing that natural food will be more plentiful here. And nothing is so important in a skunk's life as a bountiful food supply. About three months out of every year, during mid-winter, the skunk hibernates in a snug, grass or leaf-lined den, only venturing into the open if an unusual warm period arrives. Therefore, great layers of fat must be accumulated during the summer and fall, to keep the spark of life kindled while the body lies dormant. Hence the reason that plenty of food is essential to the welfare of this little black and white animal.

The food of the skunk varies somewhat in different sections of the country, but of all the natural foods that has the greatest appealing power to this animal, the writer has found that turtle's eggs and lizards lead the rest. Insects and grubs constitute the main food of the skunk, however, for the delicacies just previously mentioned are not always to be found. Field mice, birds, fowls, frogs, and the flesh of its own race are all classed as legitimate food.

The natural haunts of the skunk are sandy hillsides, brushy slopes, and rocky regions. It never burrows deep enough to make a home for itself, but occupies abandoned fox dens, woodchuck dens, rock crevices, hollow logs, or spaces under abandoned buildings. If it finds a cotton-tail rabbit in a den that it wishes to use, it speedily kills or drives out the former dweller. During the fall and summer, the animals seldom live in the same den for long periods, but rather keep moving from place to place, apparently going into the closest den when daylight threatens to arrive. This applies especially during the fall months. It seems that an old skunk is aware of the exact location of every den in his section, and even if the snow is three feet deep, it can dig down to the entrance with never a mistake. They seldom ever pass an open den without entering and coming out of a different exit if there is such. This may seem foolish to those who do not know skunks, but the reason for this is, there are apt to be crickets and other vermin hiding in its depths, which make good eating.

Along waterways are not natural dwelling places for the skunk, but when out roaming about they follow these to a great extent, knowing that grubs, insects, and turtle's eggs are apt to be plentiful here. Occasionally I have known skunks to live in great swamps, evidently preferring to live in these places. I believe that these are from generations that dwelled in swamps until they had slightly different habits than the average of the species. They made their homes under rotted stumps and when out hunting food, waded water as readily as a mink.

The tracks of a skunk resemble those made by the house cat somewhat, but they are narrower, the claws show more, and the footprints are much closer together. The skunk usually walks when going about, but will sometimes lope along in a manner peculiar to its species. It can cover great distances in a comparatively short space of time, and I have known an old male to travel more than five miles in one night. In the spring, when the animals are thin and can travel easy, it is almost impossible to track one in.

One of the commonest methods of taking the skunk up to a few years ago was to dig them from their dens with a pick and spade. Many states now prohibit this method, and no real sportsman nor any trapper that concerns himself about the future trapping industry, will indulge in it. At the time that it was practiced greatly, people were of the belief that fur-bearers were so plentiful that there could never be any shortage. After the first snowfalls, the skunk hunters located a track and followed it to the den. If it happened to be under a huge stump, or a great pile of rocks, it was passed up and another track sought. This was usually easy to find and the torturous trail was again fol-

SOME TRAPPERS DRAG A CARCASS OF CERTAIN ANIMALS AS A SCENT TO LURE FUR BEARERS TO THEIR TRAPS

lowed. If it went in and out a great many holes and ended up where they started, proving that the animal had traveled in a circle, it was up to the trapper to pick the den where the fur-bearer lived. If he was an expert skunker, he would know by dried grass and leaves far down in the hole, proving that den lining had been taken in.

Late in the season, the skunk seeks a den for the hibernation period. This is located in a spot which will not freeze through. Often it will be located in a dense woods where the leaves keep the ground warm. Thick berry and other bushes answer quite as well, or an abandoned fox den that extends below the frost limit is often used. Under old barns where there is an abundance of chaff and other dry material is an ideal winter den. In the northern sections the fur of the skunk is prime by Nov. 15th. Earlier than this, the pelt is apt to turn to a bluish shade after it has been on the stretching board a few days. This means that the skin will grade down one grade, or if very blue must be thrown down two or more.

If the trapper is not very careful in skinning the animal, much fat will be left on the hide. This absolutely must be removed when the skin is stretched or it will ruin the whole pelt. There is a pink lining between the skin proper and the fat layer. As the pelt attains primeness, this should be left attached to the animal rather than to the skin. By doing this, but little fat will adhere.

## SETS

A person who intends trapping skunk will cover his territory at least once each month during the summer and once a week during the fall. He will then know where the animals are feeding, where the young are raised, what dens they are using most, and where the regular runs are. He may increase his catch 100 per cent if he puts out bait early and replaces it as it is eaten. This method will give one a great advantage over his competitors, and the bait can be placed in hidden spots where other trappers and sneak thieves will not easily locate the sets.

I know of no fur-bearer that is better protected against natural enemies than the Skunk. Located in a gland at the root of the trail is a fluid which when emitted, gives off a very unpleasant odor and causing an intense burning sensation if a particle lodges in the eye. Many other animals are equipped with a scent which it throws when attacked or angered, but none equals the skunk when it comes to disagreeableness. Therefore this little animal usually has its right of way when traveling about. Even a dog must be trained to kill skunk, and it will long remember the first encounter. Due to the stench, few other animals care to eat the flesh of a skunk. This is one reason why they are plentiful today. If a 'coon-hunting hound tackles a skunk and gets scented, it almost ruins his power of detecting other animal trails by the aid of smell, for some hours. Occasionally a huge owl will attack and kill a skunk, but this is practically the only natural enemy of the skunk, excepting man.

The skunk likes company of its own species and if there are many of these animals living in one section, they will den together as much as possible, as the season gets late. It is evident that they realize that it will be warmer if more than one occupies a den. Occasionally there are old males that will not tolerate any other males in the den, and sometimes they fight even until death claims the weakest.

---

Methods of trapping the skunk may be divided into three classes: den sets, bait sets, and blind sets. Den sets are the commonest and as successful as any, however the trapper must be able to distinguish the difference between a den that the animals are using, and an ordinary woodchuck or rabbit den. It is commonly believed that a den occupied by skunks can be detected by "skunk odor." This is never true, for the animals do not emit scent unless attacked or angered greatly. Ordinarily they are as free from odor as a house cat. In early fall which is the usual time the prospective skunk trapper saunters across the back pastures with a string of iron dogs over his shoulder, a skunk den can be told by grass pulled in the direction of the entrance for a distance of four or five feet back. The skunk enters the den backward at this time of year and scrapes grass and leaves in for den lining. Signs of skunk are located by noting small holes extending into the ground for a few inches. These holes are tiny excavations left when removing an insect, mouse, or turtles' eggs. If the hole was dug for eggs, it will extend deeper than for the others, and bits of shell will be found nearby. After a rain which causes mud, tracks can be detected in old cowtrails, plowed furrows and in ditches.

After locating a den, the trapper is ready to make a set. A trap should be selected that has some appliance on the jaw to prevent the animal from gnawing free. For just as soon as the leg which is in the trap becomes numb, the animal will start chewing. Many persons have told the writer that they can catch skunks easily, but lose more than half by having them eat their feet. The skunk trap should be fastened to a light clog. One reason for this is that a movable clog will tend to keep the animal in the trap longer than a solid one. The other is that it can be removed from the den for killing, without going close. A long light pole is the right thing. The usual method writer advises the amateur skunk trapper to carry his catch to a stream or pond and there sink it under water until it is drowned. This is claimed to be an odorless method. Now in the first place, skunks are often caught miles from water deep enough to drown one, and second, the trapper will usually create more odor in this manner than in any other. If any trapper thinks this method of killing is practical, just try it a few times. Even if it were a good way to avoid odor, the skins would be soaking wet, and the scent gland would be so full that it would be impossible to remove the skin without squeezing some of the fluid out. The writer, after trapping and killing thousands of skunks, finds that the best method of killing is to shoot the animal directly between the eyes with a small calibre pistol or rifle. I have known a few old skunkers to bleed skunks and other fur-bearers with their knives. This leaves the skin a purer white than any other way of killing. Some claim that a sharp blow on the back will paralyze the animal to such extent that it cannot emit any scent. A few experiments will

A STRIPED KITTY OUT FOR AN EVENING STROLL

prove that this too is without foundation. If the animal is shot from a distance of fifteen feet, there is little danger of getting scented. It can then be hung up in a tree, preferably a dense evergreen where others will not find it, for twenty-four hours, when almost every trace of the hated odor will be gone.

The trap should never be set far down in the den or the animal will set it off with its body, and only a few long hairs will be the result. If the den is believed to be one that is not occupied, it is sometimes a good idea to place the trap on the outside, for occasionally an animal will circle about such den and not enter. If the weather is cold, an excavation should be made and this lined with dry material and the trap placed on top. This will prevent freezing down. It is not necessary to cover a skunk trap, a little natural cover however will do no harm. If there are two den entrances, it is best to place a trap in each one, or else block one up. If a skunk gets caught and gets free, it will invariably come out at another hole, or if there is no other, it will often dig up from the den. This proves that the animal is endowed with reasoning power. If there are many skunks in a den and one gets caught, the others are liable to kill and devour it. Visit your traps regular to prevent this.

Bait sets are used extensively in trapping the skunk. Often there are sections which have skunk signs about, but no good-looking den can be found, or it may be the trapper has no time to search for hidden dens. A piece of flesh bait of any kind hung up and a trap placed beneath it, and a little to one side is quite sure to make a catch. After one of the animals is caught, the carcass can be used for bait, and the others can smell this carcass for long distances and will come to feed on it. I know of successful skunk trappers who use the bait set altogether. A few use fish oil on the bait as a lure, but the writer never has found this essential. Others drag a piece of bait from one set to another. This may work in some instances. The greatest advantage of bait trapping is that the sets can be hidden away from others. Skunk trapping is usually carried on in territories where competition is brisk, hence the value of being able to make one's sets just where he wants them. If any dead cows or horses are lying about, as there usually is around the farmlands in the fall, this is the place to look for skunks. Small traps should be used which will not hold the farmer's dogs, for the enmity of the land-owner must never be gained. Most farmers are glad to have the skunk trapped off their farm, and often they will even allow trapping under their barns if approached right, for nearly all of them lose chickens and the skunk is usually blamed. It is not above visiting the chicken-yard.

Blind sets will sometimes pick up skunks where the trapper did not know there was any. Often they are caught in fox sets that are made in cow-trails, holes under fences, etc.

Some states prohibit trapping the skunk in the spring. This is a good law unless the animals are thick enough to constitute a nuisance. They are easier trapped in the spring than at any other time. Thinned up by their long winter's fasting, they come out every night and make long trips in search of food. The mating instinct is now strong and this causes them to move about considerable. Bait must now be hidden from crows or one of these black fiends will be found flapping about in the trap. Woodchucks begin to move in early spring, and this hurts skunk trapping some. The skins too are shrunken at this time and the fur has lost much of its fine lustre.

The color of the skunk varies with the different sections of the country. The western states and some of Canada have almost all long narrow stripes of white. Some parts of Canada have a larger percentage of whites than any other color. A black skunk or a number 1 as to color is one that has a small amount of white on the head and neck and a white tip on the tail. A good grader will take a large prime skunk as a number 1 if a narrow white stripe extends nearly halfway down the back. There is no such thing as a quarter stripe as to grading, although some buyers try to get a part of the blacks by this method. A number 2 skunk as to color is one that the stripe does not extend the full length of the back. A 3 or full stripe is a skunk that has a narrow stripe of white extending the full length of the skin. A 4, or broad-stripe, is a wide stripe extending to the tail. There is more chance for argument when selling or buying skunk skins than any other fur-bearer, on account of there being more grades. Some houses buy as to size as well as to color and primeness. Never ship very green skunk pelts a long distance or they will be liable to spoil in transit.

# CHAPTER IX

## THE MINK

### RANGE AND HABITS

MINK trapping is one of the best bets in the vocation of toe-pinching. This animal is quite equally distributed throughout every section that has any amount of waterways. It likes solitude and the silences better than the farming territories, but will be found anywhere where there is natural food. The food consists of frogs, fish, birds up to the size of a grouse, young muskrats, and mussels or clams.

One of the chief habits of the mink and one taken advantage of by the wise trapper, is that it invariably makes the same runs, and once a track is located, the animal is sure to come back. It will also visit the exact spots and will go under every stump, log, or overturned tree that is on its line. This is done in search of food. If a dead muskrat is located or other food that cannot be eaten at once, the animal will den nearby in a hollow log or stump, and return regularly until the food is exhausted. The mink seldom walks when moving about, but usually lopes, jumping around eighteen inches, and leaving the four imprints rather close together. A large mink will measure thirty inches from tip to tip.

The fur is darker in early winter and is therefore more valuable at that time. The young are

E. J. DAILEY WITH A TRAPPED MINK

born in May in most sections, the number varying with the age of the female. The den where the young are raised is usually located along the shores of a stream or near a pond or lake. It may be in an abandoned muskrat den, under a rock, or in a hollow log or stump. The trapper should never destroy one of these dens, for the animals use the same one for years if it is not molested, and a trapper with many natural mink dens in his section is in position to make a goodly amount of money each year, and this will go on indefinitely if he uses good judgment and does not trap too close.

The mink hibernates to some extent in the northland, usually during the month of January. Even during this time it moves about occasionally. If the snow is very deep, it will make tunnels underneath and travel about in this manner. If there is an abundance of warm springs where natural food may be procured the winter through, the animal sometimes remains active the whole season.

Mink are not hard to hold in a trap, for their legs consist of tough tissues, and rarely does a trapper find a wring off in a mink trap.

They move about considerably under ice, and one must be proficient in this kind of trapping to take the greatest number.

### PRACTICAL TRAPPING METHODS

It is commonly believed that the mink is a very elusive fur-bearer and equal to the fox or otter in cunning. The fact is that they are caught as easily as muskrats by trappers that study their habits and use a little common sense. It is also the belief of some that the southern mink is wiser and harder to trap than its northern brother. I think that this belief arises from the fact that water conditions are not so satisfactory for mink trapping in southern sections as some others, and the best and most successful mink sets are all made under water. The best mink trapping that I have ever experienced was in a certain section of the Adirondacks. When I started to trap at this place, it was a common thing after a fresh snow, to see the tracks of a dozen different animals on the following morning along the river bank ten rods from my cabin home. I have seen mink trails worn deep in partly dry stream beds that had flowed into the Red River of The North, but these animals did not have the dark, silky fur of our northern New York mink. In size they were considerably larger.

Blind sets work better for mink than any other kind, as natural food is nearly always easily procured by the animal. If this is scarce, then bait in the form of flesh will lure them. Birds, muskrat carcasses, fish, or rabbits are the usual baits. Anise oil and musk is used by some for a call scent.

When a prospective mink trapper locates a stream with mink tracks or other sign along it, he will go along the bank or shoreline until he comes to a rock or tree at the water's edge which will force the animal to take water. This is a natural set and one usually productive. The number 1 or 115X trap is sufficiently large for mink. They are easily drowned and the trap chain should be staked out in deep water when possible. Around old bridges are good locations for mink sets as every one traveling a stream will investigate these. If these bridges are made of logs, there are sure to be sets under

A MINK MIXED UP WITH A TRAP

them, or if stone, which they often are in the farm country, they are equally as good. Overnight stops are made at old bridges. If the trap is set on dry land, it will be necessary to cover with dry soft material like moss or cat-tail fluff. Grass or dry leaves will do.

Beaver dams are the best places in the wilderness to look for sets and signs. If there is shallow water at these places, always make the sets in this. Old partly rotted hay or straw stacks adjacent to streams are sure to be visited by these wandering animals. If there are holes underneath, a trap should be concealed at these places. Drain tiles are sought by mink and traps should be placed at the end.

When bait is used, the trapper may build a bait pen or locate a natural one. Sometimes a hole is dug about a foot back in the bank of a stream and just at the water's edge. The bait is then placed in the back and the trap in the water at the front.

A simple bait set is made by sticking a stick into the bottom of a shallow stream and placing bait on the end, which should be about ten inches above water. Then a trap is placed on either side and about one foot back. I do not recommend this for old or trap-shy animals.

The spring branch set is my favorite and is good the whole season through. Almost every stream is made up of springs that come together and form the larger body. In these narrow running springs are the best set locations. If a narrow place is located where a mink will absolutely be obliged to pass over the trap that is the proper location for the set. If no such spot is located, it may be narrowed by sticks or other material, but no freshly cut sticks should be used. Traps that lay in spring water should be sprung at least every two weeks, for they seem to "set" after this time and will fail to function properly.

Mink may be tracked in after a fresh snowstorm. They will run ten miles in a night at times, but often cover not more than one mile. After the track ends under a stump or elsewhere, it is only necessary to cover a trap at the hole, or if there are more than one, put a trap at each or block up all but one. I was setting out a line of traps in the 'Dacks one time, and I was trying to make an old camp by a roaring stream by dark, as I wished to stay overnight. I had not been at this camp for two years and I was not sure that it was in condition for a person to spend a winter night within it. As I hurried on, I came to the track of a giant mink, and as it was apparently going my way, I followed it. It played about an old skid-way and I dropped a trap in, and went on. Arriving at the cabin, I was surprised to find that the mink had gone under the floor and had not come out. I placed in a bunch of traps and shortly after dark I heard a squealing and went out to find the animal fast. At another time I was traveling up the Moose Pond outlet in the Ampersand section of the Adirondacks, and I noticed among others, a very fresh looking mink track. It was about noon and I set a trap under a shelving bank where the high water had washed away much of the dirt. It was free of snow here and was a nice location for a set. I put dry moss under the pan, and sprinkled sand over the trap. Then I went on up to the pond and looked at some

MAKING A SET IN THE END OF A PARTLY SUBMERGED LOG.
GOOD FOR MINK AND 'RATS

otter traps. On the way back, I just happened to look at the trap and a nice mink awaited me. This was not over two hours after I had set the trap. Another time a mink got to visiting the spring back of the cabin where I got my drinking water. I guess there were a few frogs in it, at least the mink pulled one up on the snow and partly devoured it. I had a couple of old traps in camp that I did not have out, and I set them in the edge of the water. It wasn't a week before I had the visitor.

In muskrat trails in the marshes are likely set locations, also around unused 'rat houses or even on the top of occupied dwellings. Under old rail fences one will often locate the runs of mink.

Few people realize that a mink can climb easily, but one day I was returning to camp, when a large one crossed a trail in front of me. I had a pack of traps and I rushed after it as fast as possible, only to see it start up a giant elm tree, going to the very top and waving back and forth in the breeze. Unluckily I had used up all my ammunition and I surrounded the tree with traps and hurried to camp for more cartridges. I had more than two miles to go, and I was detained looking for the ammunition, but when I arrived back at the tree, the animal had not moved from its original position. I waited until the wind lulled, and made a careful shot, getting it in the head which did not materially injure the fur.

The hollow log set is very good and if such log can be located in mink territory, a trap concealed at the end will take mink either with or without bait. Personally, I do not use bait for this kind of a set, for the traveling animal will investigate every hollow log on his route to make sure that no legiti-

TRAPPED MINK

mate food in the way of mice, frogs, or other small wood's being are hidden there. If fresh, bloody bait is used, one is quite sure to catch a weasel, which is not always to be desired, especially at a good mink set.

Very often a trapper will take mink in his muskrat sets, the under water traps usually catching these. If the time is fall or winter, this is to be desired, but in late spring, one should always let any mink that he catches go free if they are alive, for the faded, rubbed fur would not bring more than the price of a 'rat skin, and often it is a female that becomes tangled in your set at this time, and no sane thinking trapper would kill a female mink which would be the equivalent of killing a half dozen, for a paltry dollar or two.

A mossy log laying over a stream is a good place to locate a set for mink as well as other fur-bearers that I have mentioned in other chapters. Like fox and other sly fur-bearers, the mink is easier taken in traps that are snowed under to the extent of about two inches. Rain, too, improves the land sets.

Mink have a habit of moving more directly after a storm, and the sets should be in good condition at this time.

A professional trapper, working a good mink section, should be able to take care of one hundred traps. I know of a few such trappers that catch as many mink during the season. At an average of ten dollars each, this makes a nice winter's pay. One must be experienced and be in a section where mink are fairly plentiful to do this.

The skin of the mink should be stretched long and narrow in proportion to the unskinned animal.

The stretcher, if of wood, should be smooth and tapered at either side. Wire stretchers are to be preferred on account of better air circulation.

The claws should be left on the skin and the tail-bone removed. This bone will slip out readily if ripped one-third of the way and the skin slid off with two fingers or a split stick. In warm weather it may be necessary to split the skin to the point or at least make an insertion at the point to allow drainage. This also applies to other fur-bearers. The head should be skinned carefully and as small openings as possible left where the eyes and ears are located.

The skins grade as to color as well as to size, the darker skins bringing the most money. The pelt should be a pinkish color with no black spots in evidence, to grade as prime. The time of primeness will vary with the different sections.

## CHAPTER X

### THE SLY OTTER

"Never borrow or lend any money on the prospects of the next morning's catch."—DAILEY.

#### HAUNTS AND HABITS

THE otter is an animal of the long trails. It is here today and gone tomorrow. Few states offer it any protection due to the fact that it commits grave depredations among the trout family, yet despite this fact, its own elusiveness is ample protection, and it is found in every section where the encroachments of civilization have not taken away its natural environment.

The otter is an animal measuring from two to four feet in length. It is a sort of cross between a mink and a fur-seal. It can move about almost as readily under water as above, and can catch a muskrat with ease, which it often does. The legs are short and the feet large and sprawling, being partly webbed.

Unlike the fisher and marten, the otter will sometimes hang around in proximity to civilization, and I have seen tracks within one mile of a town of five thousand inhabitants. It is a common thing for bathers in the lakes of the Adirondack regions to become terribly frightened when one of these silky denizens suddenly thrusts its head above water close by. The first impression of such people is that the animal is of the shark family, and even the press has mentioned that certain ponds were infested with these man-killers.

The animal makes its home in dens underneath the ground, close by a pond, lake, or stream. If the bank is steep adjacent to the den, the otter will have a slide where they get much enjoyment coasting down the slippery incline into the water, in much the same manners as persons shoot-the-chute at Coney Island, Dominion park and other beach resorts. Back from the den will often be found a playground, and here the trails will be worn deeply into the ground. These dens are only occupied during the mating season and while rearing the young. Later, the animals start their roaming and it is common for one to cover twenty miles in a night. Like the mink, they are inquisitive and will work around every beaver dam that they come to. If it is winter, they never fail to go through any hole that there may be in the ice of streams, and will invariably travel underneath until another hole is arrived at.

Few trappers ever try to trail an otter with the thought of getting close to it, yet I shot a beauty one afternoon while following its track. I was trapping in Southern St. Lawrence county, in the vicinity of Cranberry Lake, and while making the rounds of my mink line, I came to the fresh imprints of an otter's feet. He came over a mountain range from some other waterway and was heading in the same direction as myself. I had the carbine with me, although this was unusual for me. The animal slid down every incline he came to and seemed to figure out his route so that he could slide much of the time. I saw that it was heading for a tiny

FAMOUS ADIRONDACK TRAPPER MAKING AN OTTER SET

mountain pond where my mink traps were set. When I got to the pond, I saw that the animal had gone under the ice at an air-hole, and I was looking in my pack to see if I had a 315 with me, when looking up I saw a movement out on the ice near the middle of the pond. It was the otter, and no sooner did I see it than it scented me and dashed for another hole where it had come out. I do not boast of being a good shot, and it may have been an accident, but that night after the sour dough cakes were prepared, I stretched the skin of the beautiful animal.

Habits of otter as well as other fur-bearers will differ in the various sections of the country and general environment. All animals adapt themselves somewhat to circumstances, therefore writers and naturalists often differ on certain points and yet both be right.

. The otter has a double coat of fur, and like the beaver, the coarse must be removed before the under or finer coat may be viewed in all its beauty. Sometimes it is made up in the original state, and then at a later date, the owner can have a change by the process of "plucking."

The animal is rather hard to take in steel traps, and still harder to hold after it is caught, unless the catch is made close to deep water where the drowning system will work. Traps with teeth on the jaws are used extensively, for it is hard to get a good leg grip. I caught one in an ordinary muskrat trap at one time, however. I had the trap set on a log for 'rats and when I left the set, the trap was slightly above the level of the water. That night it rained and the water rose above the trap.

The log lay across a narrow stream, and the animal was either swimming up or down the stream or else it attempted to cross over on the log. The trap happened to get a good foothold and winding the chain around the log, it soon drowned. I was much surprised when I pulled the animal from the stream.

### TRAPPING METHODS

Water sets are the only kind worth considering for the otter. Being naturally suspicious, and frightened at the odor of man, land sets can only be used successfully by trappers who have had much experience and know the art of land set making, with the complete elimination of foreign scent.

Probably more otter are taken at their slides or rather at the come-back path than in any other set. If a slide is located, look for the place where the animal leaves the water and place a powerful trap underneath. It is much better to make the set from a boat, which will not molest the surroundings. If this is impossible, then wade with rubber boots so as to leave no odor. The trap should be staked in deep water.

A favorite Adirondack otter set is to fence off a stream with heavy sticks, leaving only one opening. This must be done in summer. Then in trapping season, place in the trap. This set has one failing, it is apt to take traveling beaver, which are protected every month but March. 'Coons often get mixed with an otter set also.

An abandoned beaver dam is sometimes cut so that a passing otter will have but one opening to go through, and a trap placed at this point.

If a stream takes a sharp bend, an otter will in-

ENTRANCE TO DEN USED BY OTTER

variably take a short cut across. Where the tracks show the point where it leaves the stream is a good set location. Some trappers use a mixture of beaver castor, otter musk, and fish oil as a lure, but I do not particularly advise the use of any artificial scent for this animal.

Occasionally, trappers make bait sets for otter. A fish or a muskrat is best for this purpose, being natural food. Frogs or clams are also used. An old muskrat den close to the water's edge makes the best bait pen, and the trap should be under water. This is almost a mink method, but any good mink set will be fair for otter also, with the exception that the trap must be more powerful.

Sometimes a hole is cut in the ice and if there is a space between, a fish is either suspended or impaled or a stick and traps set near by. The hole is then covered over with a block of snow or ice so that the set will not freeze.

Spring branches which do not freeze are good locations to place otter traps, and close to the shore where there is a jutting point extending into the water, or where a large rock forces the animal into the water when it is moving along the shore.

Once an otter track is located, one can depend that it will be back in the vicinity within three weeks. It is hard work however, keeping the trap in working order during this time, especially if the weather is cold.

Sometimes two or more otter will travel together seemingly enjoying each other's company, and during the summer, a dozen or more old ones will often locate at one small pond. When this happens, it is useless to try and catch many fish from this pond.

Few American trappers trap for otter alone, and a person that catches a dozen of them in one season would have to be in an exceptionally good section. Here in the 'Dacks they are pursued early in the season when but little other trapping is allowed, and then after the 'rat season during late spring.

Two dozen traps are about all any one individual could place in this section to an advantage, and only the best sections could accommodate this amount.

The animal hibernates during January in the north, or else stays under the ice where it finds food. During February, it takes the trails again and covers the greatest distances at this time.

Snow sets may be used when water is not available, but like other snow trapping, one's luck depends on the elements. The trap should be snowed over and then not visited closely. If the trap remains in working condition until the otter comes back, a catch is assured if the trap is properly placed.

On top of beaver dams are the best places to allow one's traps to snow under, and bait should not be used. A heavy clog should be used for fastening the trap or the animal will chew free and escape with the trap.

# CHAPTER XI

## THE BEAR

### RANGE AND HABITS

THE bear is the play-boy of the woods. When one or more are about in their natural haunts, they are constantly rolling about, walking on their hind legs, and committing pranks of every sort. Of course there are instances where they have shown fight, and a few persons have passed over the divide where none returns, by encountering one of them in an angry mood. However, only a wounded bear, or a female with young will attack a person.

A hunter and trapper was killed by a bear in the fall of 1924. He was a Finn, and lived in the woods near English River, New Ontario. The trapper was a powerful man, but he was rather inexperienced in the ways of the wilds. One morning he went to his traps. When he failed to return on the third day, searching parties were organized, and his body was found near his trapline. Claw-marks and broken bones told the story, and there were tufts of hair from a bear still clutched in the trapper's hands. Evidently the trapper had wounded the animal with his rifle and it rushed him. At close quarters he apparently wielded his trapping axe and the bear left a bloody trail, but the trapper was no match for the pain-crazed animal and it quickly crushed out his life.

Under ordinary circumstances, a bear will run from a person as readily as a deer, and it takes an expert trailer to get close enough to shoot one, even if there is a good tracking snow. In the Adirondack region it is not uncommon for a party of deer hunters to drive one or more from a mountain-side when making a "drive" for deer. I have often seen them jump from a leaning tree, and make off hot foot, when I was following the trapline.

There are many species of bear, ranging from the great Alaskan bear, to the little black bear of the States. Almost every section has its own type of bears. They make their home in rocky caverns, under great shelving rocks, or under large evergreen trees, which have low branches that touch the ground, leaving a space underneath. Under a windfall is a common den in the 'Dacks.

The food of the bear consists of roots, berries, honey, or fruit, and occasionally flesh or insects and grubs, including lizards. They are also fond of fish, especially the polar bear, which has to depend on this diet almost exclusively, unless a seal is located. Being white, the polar bear is hard to distinguish against the background of snow, and a seal lying near his diving place cannot see him until he is close. The seal sleeps fitfully, taking about five minutes for each nap. The bear remains motionless while the seal is awake, which is told by constant motion of the fins. Then when it sleeps again he advances until he gets close enough for a rush. The northern hunter uses the same methods as the bear when hunting seals.

Many doubtful tales are circulated regarding bears. There is one that always appeals to me as humorous. An old trapper was supposed to have been out in the Adirondack forest building a deadfall for bear. After completing the trap, he attempted to pass under the huge log to put some honey that he carried in a pail in the back part of the pen. In some manner the trap was sprung, and the log pinned the trapper to the earth, resting across his legs. The honey pail dropped and tipped, the contents running over the trapper's feet. In vain the man struggled, until night came on. Then out of the deep forest came a sound. It was a bear approaching. The trapper was filled with a terrible fear. Coming close, the animal sniffed the honey and began licking the ground. When all the sweet was partaken of that was mixed with the earth, the bear began to remove it from the legs and feet of the trapper. It even pulled his honey-soaked shoes and stockings from his feet, and after devouring them, began licking the man's feet. Surely this was a rare and none the less terrible experience to be pinned under a deadfall, while a wild bear licked one's very feet. As the story was told, the trapper's partner finding that his bunk-mate did not return, took the trail the following morning and found the trapper devoid of reason.

Another tale was of a Dutchman that had a tame bear. The animal was much thought of by its owner. One night the pet escaped into the woods and failed to come back. Some time later, a bear was driven away from a sheep that it had just killed and the person told the Dutchman that he was sure it was the pet that he had chased from its victim. The man was very glad to hear from his former pet and resolved to get it back. That night

BRUIN TAKES A DRINK

he took a coil of rope and hid close by the slaughtered sheep, to make sure of his hold, the man tied one end of the rope about his body. It was a moonlight night and soon a dark shadow came in the direction of the sheep. Carefully the Dutchman coiled the rope and sure was his throw. The rope settled squarely and then tightened. Quickly the poor Dutchman was yanked from his feet and dragged off. In vain he called to his supposed pet to stop, but when it failed to do this he knew that a mistake had been made. It was not the pet, but a wild bear that he had caught with the rope. After being terribly bruised he managed to get his knife from his pocket and cut the rope.

For many years, bear hunters have operated in the Adirondack Mountains in a professional way. There always has been a good demand for live bear to keep around summer resorts as pets, and for other purposes, and a lively cub often brought one hundred dollars. Up till recently, the animal was not protected by law, and hunters made large sums in the spring and summer. It was no easy trick bringing in a half grown bear alive, and these hunters could always show many a scar made by sharp claws.

Bear were used as much for food as any other animal by the old time trappers of every section. The flesh is tough and dry at the best, yet it would keep well, and the fat was used for everything from a spread for bread or doughnut making, to greasing one's boots. They were always covered with a thick layer of fat in the fall, the same as every other fur-bearer that hibernates for long periods.

## TRAPPING METHODS

Blind and bait sets are both used for trapping the bear, but in localities where persons or cattle are apt to be about, it is advisable to stick to the bait pen set altogether.

A bait pen for bear is made in a V shape and fastened securely at the back so that the animal cannot get at the bait there. The bait usually consists of singed flesh in connection with honey or fruit. The size of trap needed will vary greatly with the different sections. It should be concealed in front of the pen and fastened to a heavy clog, but not to a perfectly solid object.

Trail sets are made in paths used by the animals in going to and from certain places. A wild apple tree will be visited regularly in a bear section if there is any fruit on it. Sometimes a carcass of a large animal will be visited and traps should be placed in the trails.

The same trail is often used by bear in the woods, and oft-times a trail will be located that is blazed by the animals scratching the bark from trees as high as they can reach. These old paths are good set locations if no persons are about.

It is a common occurrence for bear to visit lumber camps where lard tubs, pork barrels, and other refuse is thrown out. I knew of four bear being taken within ten rods of a lumber camp, after they got to feeding. Bears seemingly are fond of pork, and I have known them to take a good size hog from pens of settlers near the edge of the big woods.

Few animals are harder to kill than a bear. The muscles are knotted and tough, and the fat fills up the wound. Even a trapped bear should be shot with a high powered rifle, unless the trapper is a professional and knows his business. I heard of a bear swinging a trap and clog into the air and bringing it down on a trapper's head, when he ventured too close.

Bear traps should always be picked up when one is through using them. I knew of a person stepping in a rusty bear trap in mid-summer that had been set since the season before. This unfortunate individual carried the great trap many miles through the forest until he came to a settlement, and it was attached to his leg.

The bear is skinned "open," and all fat should be scraped off. Bear skins usually bring a good price, but they are heavy and hard to pack out of the far back places.

## CHAPTER XII

### THE BUSY BEAVER

#### HABITS AND HABITAT

THE beaver is an interesting animal. A few years ago, they were all but extinct. Then closed seasons were brought about and sections where there were none were restocked from forest reserves. Today the animals are found in fairly plentiful numbers in many states of the Union and in about every province in Canada.

The beaver is a water animal weighing around fifty pounds for a large one. In their natural state they appear to be covered with coarse unattractive fur, but when the outside coat is removed by plucking, a beautiful, dark, glossy inner-fur is seen. There is no better wearing fur than that possessed by the beaver, and in the early days, they were sought more than any other fur-bearer in the New World, and their trading value was higher than any other.

The beaver resembles a muskrat somewhat in looks and habits. The front feet are small, and the back feet large and sprawling with partly webbed feet. The teeth are scissor-like and capable of taking great bites from trees.

The food of the beaver consists mainly of barks, twigs, and other vegetation. Poplar, birch, and alders seem to be preferred to any other. In the fall the animals cut and store large quantities of food, and even at that they sometimes run out and are obliged to come out in mid-winter and collect a new supply. When they do this they invariably locate a spot where there is a huge snowbank at the water's edge. At this point there will be only a little ice and the animals know this. Then too, the hole will not freeze over quickly under the snow. When traveling on land in search of food the animals use a regular trail, only branching when the object of their search is located.

Like the common muskrat there are two types of beaver: the bank or stream beaver, and the house or marsh beaver. They differ only in environment, but different trapping methods should be used.

The stream beaver selects a tiny stream and after locating a favorable spot where considerable food is available, prepares with the help of others to dam it, raising the water to a desired level usually five or six feet. Then two or three counter dams are built below this one making everything quite secure against water loss. Then if the banks of the stream are high enough so that a portion is above water, they proceed to dig dens with entrances below water.

The house beaver is found in swampy sections, and here too the animals build dams, sometimes a quarter of a mile in length. These dams are built mainly of small logs, mud, and reeds. The animals roll the logs to the water and float them to the desired position. Four beaver will move a log as large as any man could move.

The animals live in colonies, and when they get too plentiful the young search out new locations

SHOOTING A TRAPPED ADIRONDACK BEAVER

(123)

and prepare for a new home. Beaver castors are highly prized by many as a scent ingredient. They are found at the root of the tail. The tail is large and filled with oil. They are eaten with apparent relish by extreme northerners. The writer never could bring himself to devouring any part of the tail, but the flesh of the animal is fine eating, being short grained and tender. Some trappers drag a beaver tail about over their traplines, claiming that it lures certain fur-bearers.

The animal uses this broad tail as a trowel when plastering up dams and houses. It also gives a warning by slapping the water, causing a resounding crack.

The beaver lodge or house is built not unlike a giant 'rat house. There may be two or three apartments. Food is usually stored in the lower or second one. Sometimes the lodge will be built on land that is not covered with water but boggy. Then tunnels will be dug to the water where the dam entrance will be located. There may be two or more of these entrances. No cold blast can freeze through one of these homes of the wilderness engineers.

While usually found in the wilds and mountainous regions, the beaver will sometimes be found close to human habitations. For many years, none of the animals were found in the St. Lawrence River, then one spring a few fresh cuttings were found around the islands north of Saint Lawrence County, New York State. Nearly all these islands had summer camps on them and the owners were interested—for a while. Then cuttings became more numerous, and finally a boat house was taken over by the animals. Soon every tree on the islands was threatened and it became necessary to trap down the animals. No one could be found who claimed to have brought in the original stock, so it is believed that the animals migrated in from the Adirondack country, a distance of forty miles.

I tried to tame a beaver once, but was obliged to give it up, as it showed no signs of domestication at the end of a month, and bit my partner on the leg, lacerating it like a knife.

### SETS

The beaver is classed among the sly fur-bearers. Personally, I never found them hard to trap, unless it was an animal that had become educated by previous acquaintance with the device of steel. Water sets are the best sets when they can be used. As stated before, when the animals leave the water for food or other purposes, they invariably take a trail. At the water end of this trail is the best set location. The trap should be set under water and if the trapping can be done from a boat the set is all the more sure. It takes a large, powerful trap to hold a beaver such as the No. 3 or a number four in the lighter makes. Care should be taken in fastening the traps so that the animal will drown. If this cannot be done, a dry hardwood clog should be used, for the trapped animal will quickly chew up a green stick and escape with the trap.

Some unsportsmanlike trappers cut holes in the dam and either hide and shoot the animals when they come up to repair it or set traps in the water where they will place their feet when making the repairs.

Early fall trappers set traps where the animals leave the water when adding to the lodges or dams. Others cut holes in the lodge and place in a trap. Either method is liable to scare the beaver out of the immediate vicinity.

Den entrance sets are used for bank beaver in much the same manner as one would set for a muskrat. Feed bed sets are also used extensively. These consist of piles of cut brush and twigs from the trees that the animals prefer. Small streams may be fenced off as described for otter and mink, and these sets will take traveling beaver. Dry sticks should be used for the fencing.

At certain places on the stream banks and on hummocks which rise above the water, the beaver will deposit a certain amount of scent in the same manner the muskrat does. Other passing animals will detect this scent and climb out of the water at this point. A trap properly placed is quite sure to produce a pelt.

Winter trapping is mostly done around open places in the ice where the animals come up for food. In another chapter I have taken up "under ice trapping," which explains how to take all water animals during the period when they are closed in by walls of ice.

Under old bridges are good locations for beaver sets as the animals knowing they are hidden from their natural enemies at this point will stop to feed or climb out of the water. Bits of poplar bark and twigs are used successfully for bait, and the essence from the beaver castor and oil glands for scent.

Beaver do great damage in the way of flooding valuable timber tracts which soon die as the result. They also cause wash-outs on railroads, and sometimes ruin good fishing grounds. Adjacent to the farm country they flood meadows, and cause cattle to get mired and drowned. They will also quickly clean up an alfalfa or clover field.

Here in New York State we have an open season on beaver of one month out of the year. Thousands of dollars worth are annually taken, and some trappers catch around fifty during the month.

As few signs as possible should be left when trapping beaver. Often a whole family of these animals will vacate the natural or regular home after one animal is trapped. Whether one animal can convey a warning to others of the species after it has got free from a trap has never advanced more than a theory with me. It is a fact however that the whole species get more wise after constant trapping.

Beaver should be skinned "open," but the legs should not be ripped, but rather "peeled" off. The skin should be stretched as nearly round as possible, and this may be accomplished by tacking on a flat surface or by tying inside of a hoop made for that purpose.

The skins are graded as to size and section of the country where they were taken. Occasionally they are bought and sold at an average price, especially in large lots.

128   TRAPLINES AND TRAILS

Never set traps where there are apparently only a pair of beaver living, or you will destroy a greater chance later.

TREES CUT BY BEAVER IN THE ADIRONDACK FOREST

# CHAPTER XIII

## THE MUSKRAT

### HAUNTS AND HABITS

NO other fur-bearer is as well known as the humble muskrat, and none puts more money in the pockets of the trapper. Year after year the 'rat has led in the number of skins taken and in the value thereof. From Maine to California and from Alaska to the Gulf of Mexico, the muskrat is pursued and taken in great numbers each year, yet due to its prolificness, this fur-bearer is today found in plentiful numbers in nearly every section.

The muskrat is a habitat of the swamps, marshes, streams, ponds, lakes and lowlands. While they spend much of their time under water, their dens are made above water, and they cannot exist without air for more than a few minutes.

The muskrat might be divided into two classes: The marsh 'rat and the stream 'rat. The marsh 'rat dwells in houses made of mud, moss, reeds, sticks, and grasses. This is made in two or three apartments, one above the other, for protection from rapidly rising water. The animals not only live in these houses but store their food in them. They are so closely built that they seldom freeze to the inside, and if one is opened, even in zero weather, the interior will be found as warm as a heated dwelling. There are usually two entrances, coming in from the water. The stream 'rat dens far back under the banks, and digs holes from near the bottom of the stream to the den which is an excavation usually as large as a bushel basket. This is lined with grasses, and like the upper den in a house, is above the high water line. Occasionally the water will rise in spring above all dens and houses. At this time the animals lay around at the water's edge, or hide under stumps or logs at convenient spots. They are easily shot at this time, but shooting ruins the fur and rapidly depletes the 'rats. Some states prohibit shooting muskrats. Every state should do this.

There are apparently a half dozen species of muskrats, running from the dark 'rats of a very small size which live in the swamps to the big, brown, clam-eating 'rats of the Great Lakes region and the Saint Lawrence River. Food has much to do with the quality of the fur, and the 'rats found in the cold or wilderness sections, where natural food is scarce, are never to be compared with the 'rats of sluggish streams and marshes which always has an abundance of food at hand. The best muskrats that I ever saw, were those that fed almost entirely on frogs and clams. I have seen a half bushel of these piled up in a 'rat's den at one time.

Grasses and roots are the main food of the muskrat. The root of the sweet flag is a favorite food. The animals will eat grain if it grows adjacent to the natural home. Some trappers advise the use of apples, carrots, turnips, and other vegetables as bait, but the 'rat usually being well supplied with natural foods seldom bothers with bait. If a trapper uses bait, I advise the root of the sweet flag. A piece of this placed beside the set will sometimes

MUSKRAT HOUSE IN GOOD TRAPPING SECTION

improve it. The musk may be removed from the glands and a drop of this used as a lure, although sets that have been used considerably by the animals will already be saturated with this fluid.

Muskrats are terrible fighters and often the old males fight until the weakest is killed. Skins of the fighters often have holes in them which have been bitten through, and always there are innumerable scars of battles of the past. When a 'rat is caught in a trap and remains alive, others of the species will often chew the skin until it is ruined, but they will not eat the flesh like the skunk and some others of the midnight roamers. The muskrat has as many as three litters in one season, and seven or eight in number are not unusual. Before the young can swim about, the mother tows them, each baby 'rat holding to her breasts. The youngsters grow very rapidly, and soon are able to shift for themselves. They show the house-building instinct very early, and soon begin piling up mounds of chewed grasses in the form of a house, but usually they do not make any den in the inside. The last litter are what is known as "kits" to the fur trade. They have short, grayish fur and have but little value. Fall trapping has been discontinued in some states, due mainly to this fact, for it is a great waste to take a ten cent 'rat in the fall that would command more than one dollar in the spring.

The natural enemy of the muskrat is the mink, and where 'rats are plentiful, mink will also be found. Sometimes a mink will eat a trapped 'rat, but it usually prefers to kill its own.

During the winter, muskrats of the northland often leave the regular dens and make homes in huge snowbanks adjacent to the water. These are dug and finished in the same manner as that used by the stream 'rat in making its burrow in the banks. I have known them to chew into solid ice and make a den there.

### TRAPPING METHODS

Muskrat trapping is divided into two classes: Fall and spring, and will vary on marshes or streams. The fall trapping is more certain on account of the fact that the water holds its level better, however, the animals move about more in the springtime, especially the first week after the ice leaves, for after being penned in by ice and snow for many months, they appear very grateful to be free once more. Then there are green shoots of grass and flags starting up that are attractive in the way of food after a winter of plain roots.

The first trapping in the spring is den trapping in the snowbanks. When the first big thaws come, portions of the den thaw away. If the part is but a small opening, the dwellers quickly plug this up with lining from the den. When one of these plugged openings is located, it is only necessary to open the den, place in a trap, and cover over again. If a large hole is thawed through, the animals will invariably vacate. This set has the disadvantage of being of the dry variety, and while any 'rat is easily caught in a trap, it is one of the most difficult fur-bearers to hold in the whole list. The trapper must continually bear in mind that his catch should be made fast by the hind leg which is larger, contains more tendons, and is much harder to "wring off." Traps set in more than two inches

SETTING A TRAP IN A RUN USED BY 'RATS. MINK ARE OFTEN TAKEN IN SETS OF THIS KIND

of water will usually score a hind leg catch, and the animal will be there awaiting the next round of the trapper. If the water surrounding the set is more than one foot deep, the 'rat can often be drowned by staking the chain out at full length, and then driving another stake about one foot farther out. When the animal is caught it will swim around the outside stake, tangles itself up and soon drowns. An extension chain has many advantages in 'rat trapping. Wire devices are sometimes used for drowning muskrats, but this method takes more time than the professional 'rat trapper can spare. They consist of a long wire reaching into deep water and fastened with a stone. Notches on the wire hold the chain from coming back after it slips down. Many traps are now on the market with jaws made to prevent wringing or twisting out. Some of the best of these do aid considerably, but as the animal twists out above the jaws, it is obvious that patented jaws will not always prevent the getting free. In freezing weather the new forming ice gives the 'rat a foothold, and a correspondingly large percentage of "legs" will be the result. Different trap companies are now selling traps intended to kill the animal soon after it is caught. Some of these will do this quite regular, but all of these traps are so large and bulky that only in certain sets can they be used. A trapper can use one third of these killer traps to an advantage.

As mentioned before, rising and lowering water makes spring trapping difficult, and in some sections of the country, especially the southern part, it will rise many feet in a night during the fall as well as spring. In these sections, floating objects like stumps and logs are the surest places to make sets. A small flat-setting trap of the under-spring type is best for a log set. A quantity of grasses which has been chewed by 'rats may be packed around the trap, and a few roots of the flag placed near by. Around the bases of trees that grow adjacent to a stream are good places to look for "sign," and if any is found, a trap should be set. If any hollow logs or trees are in the vicinity of muskrat sections, these animals will often den in them, and especially if they can enter from the water. The main set of the marshes is the feeding bed set, made by placing a trap in the water near the edge of piled refuse left where the animals have a habit of feeding. A few fresh roots thrown on top the pile will improve the set. Under overhanging stream banks are sure sets, if the traps can be staked out. Huge cakes of ice that are thrown partly on the banks make shelter for the 'rats after the water lowers, taking one part of the ice with it and thus leaving a space at the edge of the bank. This applies of course to northern trapping only. It is sometimes dangerous to crawl under these great cakes weighing many tons and I have seen them fall with a loud crash.

Trails or runs leading about through a marsh are a sure bet to the trapper, and here the killer type of traps will work, in fact it is quite essential that they be used, for here is an excellent opportunity for the 'rat to escape by twisting out.

Entrances to bank dens or houses can be located when the water is clear and the light is good. A trap placed at the very entrance is well set, and a 'rat caught under water can never escape if the

ON THE TRAIL OF THE MUSKRAT

trap is staked down. If muddy water is issuing from the entrance it is a sure sign that the den is occupied, as the animals moving about disturb the dirt and cause the roily water.

During the fall trapping, the animals are continually piling material on their houses, or on top of stumps, logs, and brush-piles where they intend to spend the winter. This gives the trapper an easy chance to take them. They always use the same trail when leaving the water and carrying up the material, and a trap placed in the water at this point will hold something on each visit.

Sometimes 'rats can be driven into a trap if they live in bank dens. One time my partner and I were trapping a small stream which emptied into the Saint Lawrence River. Coming to a den entrance which was just at the water's edge, we were surprised to see a 'rat jump from the opening to the water. Thinking there might be more, one of us placed a trap carefully at the entrance and the other struck the ground with a club. When we got through there were seven of the animals laying dead on the ground. Once I was in the act of setting a trap under a stump, when a 'rat jumped from somewhere in the stump and landed in the trap which was in my hands at the time.

Then walking about in muddy places or on snow, the muskrat leaves a plain trail with its small front feet, its sprawling, webbed hind feet and the dragging tail. Occasionally they will make long trips overland, when frozen out or in need of water.

The amount of traps needed by a muskrat trapper will vary greatly. A professional 'rat trapper working in a good section can handle from three to five

SPRING 'RAT SKINS

hundred traps. A stream or mixed section trapper will not use more than two hundred. An auto trapper or motor-boat trapper will carry a few extra for an emergency, and need two hundred and fifty. The person who has a few hours of the day to spare, and lives in an average settled community, will find that fifty good traps will suffice. A trapper going into a real wilderness, will need but few 'rat traps, especially if the section be of the extreme north. The shaded wilderness and the cold swift streams are not adapted to the natural food of the 'rat, and a proper amount of food has more to do with the plentifulness of fur-bearers than any other one thing.

The heavy pelted, best grades of the northern muskrat skins are sold for fancy prices, and are made up into what is known to the trade as "Hudson Seal." Out of one hundred average spring 'rats, only about one half will be good enough for this imitation, and the buyer will know the percentage when he makes a bid. The little swamp 'rats never attain weight enough to grade top.

Muskrats should always be skinned "cased," that is, ripped from one hind leg to the other and peeled off over the body. Most 'rat trappers use wire stretchers at the present time which are sold cheaply by nearly all sporting goods dealers, fur houses, trap companies, and others. These wire stretchers allow a circulation of air to pass through when the skin is stretched, which dries the fur as well as the skin. Large, pointed shingles will suffice as stretchers. When making a stretching board for any animal, remember that it should conform in shape to the unskinned animal. For instance, the 'rat is a short thick animal and the skin needs a blunt-pointed, wide board. A mink is a long thin animal and the pelt should be stretched in the same ratio.

Muskrat skins are graded as to large, medium, and small, and some buyers quote a price on extra large. The most satisfactory method of selling skins is what is known as "flat," or counting noses. This means an average price on an entire lot, usually the method of buying in the North by country dealers. Sometimes a price is quoted "flat," with kits and very small or damaged out at value. The tails should be removed from the skins as they are without value, excepting in the case of Maryland and Delaware 'ratters who often stretch two rats on a board, one on each end and using the tails to tie the skins together.

Along the eastern coast of the United States, around the Great Lakes, and the Saint Lawrence River marshes, are the most noted 'rat sections. Portions of Alabama and Louisiana contain good marshes, but the skins of the muskrats are not as high quality as those taken farther north.

A little article known as a trap placer which is sold by nearly all fur companies, and which enables the trapper to place a trap in position under two feet of water without wetting the hands is indispensable to those pursuing muskrats. Hip boots are usually needed unless one traps from a boat only. Long rubber gloves like those used by electric linemen are a good thing for the northern 'rat trapper, and will save much suffering in the way of cold

REMOVING A TRAPPED 'RAT

hands, especially when one has to break a half inch of ice to locate the set. 'Rats which are alive should be shot with a 22-cal. pistol.

One thing that puzzles the amateur 'rat trapper is the apparent disappearance of the animals at a certain time in the spring.

Often the catch will be very good up to a particular day, and then drops off to nothing and continues this way. The trapper often believes that the animals are all caught out and pulls his traps. This is probably the proper thing to do, for the balance of the 'rats are of a high percentage of females which should be allowed to propagate.

However the animals do not leave the vicinity, excepting where food has become scarce, but rather keep almost entirely in the den or work about under water. The deep den entrances are used at this time and are hard to locate. The reason for this hibernation is that the mating season is now about over, and the animals are much more dormant. They remain thus until late in the summer when the instinct for house building awakens their latent energies.

Another 'rat puzzler is a pond that contains many houses in the fall and plentiful signs, and yet in the spring there will be no animals and no trapping done in the meantime. I attribute this to the fact that many ponds in the North freeze to the bottom during the winter, thus driving the animals away to open water or freezing them to death.

## CHAPTER XIV

### THE RACCOON

#### HAUNTS AND HABITS

THE 'coon is a native of the swamps and lowlands. It is found to some extent in almost every state in the Union and a great part of Canada. Our forefathers used the skin of the 'coon for the manufacture of coats, mittens, caps, and other apparel to a greater extent than any other fur. This was due to the fact that the skin was heavy and wore for long periods, and the fur being extremely thick, kept out the terrible cold of the North. In the heavy wooded sections where there are plenty of large trees, the 'coon usually makes its den in a hollow trunk or limb. In the swampy sections where the timber is cut off, they live under stumps or in holes in hummocks.

The 'coon is nocturnal in its habits and is rarely seen moving about in daytime. If caught far from a regular den at daylight, it will crawl under almost any shelter. It is of the long trails and will cover many miles in one night, therefore if one notices a track of this animal it is never a sure sign that the 'coon is nearby.

In some sections of the country, the raccoon is hunted and trapped for the flesh as well as the fur. Nearly all trappers save the meat, and after the fat is stripped off and the remainder baked to a nice brown, no finer dish could be imagined.

The 'coon hibernates for about four months, d
pending on the section. They usually den together
at this time and it is not unusual for a half dozen
animals to occupy one tree. If the den happens to
be in a limb or small tree, the 'coons will lay in
layers, and I have known the lower ones to be
smothered or otherwise killed. A 'coon tree can be
told by claw marks, but must look close to distinguish between these animals and grey squirrels
or porcupines. If a small tree is standing close to
the den tree, the animals will climb this more than
the larger one. A traveling 'coon will visit every
den on his route, and no tree should ever be cut
for once the dens are gone, the animals are apt to
migrate to other sections. This applies to many
other species of fur-bearers, and the wise trapper
will be continually looking ahead if the fur supply
is to be maintained. A wise farmer always saves
some seed; the wise trapper and hunter should do
likewise.

The food of the 'coon consists of insects, frogs,
wild grapes, berries, fish, clams, corn, bird's eggs,
and occasionally flesh. For some reason, whether
cleanliness or not I do not know, the 'coon invariably washes its food before it devours it. I know
of no other animal that does this.

The track of the 'coon is sprawling, the hind
foot being much larger than the front, leaves a
correspondingly larger imprint. When loping, they
place two feet close together. The tyro often mistakes the tracks of woodchucks for 'coon. The footprints are somewhat alike, but the method of placing the feet is not alike. The woodchuck being

LOOKING OVER A DEN 'COON TREE

of the squirrel family, jumps with the four feet close together. Raccoon when traveling will often climb on rail fences or logs and walk these as far as they extend in the general direction which the animal is traveling. The hind foot of the 'coon resembles in form, that of a small child.

There is no harder fighter among the animals for its size than the raccoon. A trained dog can kill one, but a dog that makes the first attack will get an awful surprise. Catlike, it fights with its claws as well as its teeth. The favorite fighting position is lying on its back. But even being a terrible fighter, it does not often attack other animals unless cornered.

The 'coon is hunted with dogs even more than it is trapped, especially in the South. These southern 'coon will run almost as far as a fox, while the northern species will tree readily. When closely cornered the animal will take water and will sometimes swim across large streams. If a dog attacks a 'coon in the water, it will try to pull the dog's nose under water and drown it. I have known of incidents where they accomplished this.

The 'coon is a very able climber. No tree is too small nor none too large for this animal to climb. I have tried to shake them out of a tree, and while this can be accomplished if conditions are favorable, it is at times impossible, if the animal has a good foothold.

I got ten 'coons out of one den tree at one time. It was late in February and one morning there was a nice, fresh tracking snow. I had a good foxhound that had been tied for a week and begged me to take the gun and stir up one of those red renegades. We located a fox track within a half mile of camp, and the hound filled the morning air with its music. The fox was an old one and entered a swamp that consisted of thousands of acres, and which was known as "Huckleberry Swamp."

I followed along slowly, noting the various animal tracks. Many skunk had been frolicking about on the fresh snow, and rabbit, squirrel, and weasel had been searching for food on the night previous. Entering the swamp, I came to the trail of a flock of 'coon. A 'coon track always interested me more than any other track of the civilization fur-bearers, and forgetting the hound and the fox, I followed the trail. Many were the den trees that were visited, but none seemed suitable until a huge ash was arrived at, which had the top broken off and apparently was hollow. I had my belt axe with me and a steel trap was in my pocket, and I climbed up. There was a solid limb near the den entrance, and standing on this I gazed into the dark hole. In the darkness, I saw the glimmer of a pair of eyes, and poking in a switch, an answering growl came back. I set the trap and let it down into the den. This was like fishing. About the third attempt, I got a strike and I pulled a struggling 'coon from the hole. One rap with the axe and I dropped it to the ground and resumed my fishing. I took nine more from the den, keeping the last one for a pet, and I had a hard time getting it down out of the tree and home without getting bitten. I did not injure the tree, and since that time, I have trapped many 'coon at its base.

The best way to learn the location of the 'coon dens in your locality, is to follow one's tracks in the springtime. Often they den within a few rods from the edge of a woods, and in a spot that has been passed by dozens of trappers and hunters and never located.

### TRAPPING METHODS

The blind or trail set is more extensively used for trapping the raccoon than any other method. Being more or less of a water animal, blind sets of the water variety may be utilized to a great extent, and water sets are much the surest for any fur-bearer than can be induced to enter it, due to the fact that water automatically eliminates all foreign odors. The prospective 'coon trapper should follow along streams until a track is located. If it enters water at a certain place, it will invariably do the same thing on the next trip. If a small stream flows into a larger one, and the branch is of very shallow water, the 'coon will wade up it for a distance in search of frogs and minnows. If a log lies across a stream, a trap at each end will often take 'coon as well as many other fur-bearers, and it is the general purpose set that makes the most money for the trapper. Make such sets with great care and elusive animals like fox and otter are often taken. If a log or tree lies partly submerged, the raccoon will crawl out on this to watch for fish and frogs, therefore a trap should be placed where the animal climbs on the log or a space may be chopped out so that the trap will be level or flush with the top and the trap set here.

The 'coon is a very aggressive animal and being a

hard fighter it takes a powerful trap to hold one. Occasionally a muskrat trap will hold one, but I heartily recommend a No. 3 trap for taking the 'coon, unless the set is made where the animal will drown, where a No. 2 may be used. The 215 trap is an ideal size, having ample gripping space and power to hold even the largest of the species. When clogging a 'coon trap it is advisable that the trapper use a movable clog as the animal will not be as apt to escape. This applies to almost every other fur-bearer. The best method of killing a trapped 'coon is to shoot it with a small calibre rifle or pistol.

Den sets are usually made at the base of a den tree or at holes in hollow logs or stumps. It is not essential that the den be occupied to make a catch for as mentioned previously, these animals visit every den adjacent to the one they are living in when they are roaming about. It is an art in itself to properly make a set at a "coon tree." One must be expert enough to know just where to place his trap, for if it were simply set beside the tree, it would take at least two dozen to go all around it and one would be as liable to catch as the other. If the tree is leaning, the animals will invariably come down or go up on the high side. The side that has the most claw-marks on it is evidently used the most. The trap should be placed at least eighteen inches from the tree as the 'coon wil jump off when it gets near the bottom. Holes near the bottom of hollow snags are good locations for sets, as a traveling 'coon will investigate these.

Sometimes the raccoon will raid a farmer's corn-

AT THE BASE OF LARGE TREES IS A GOOD SET LOCATION

field, and if it is left out until the fur is good, one can make a catch by locating the trails leading to the field and concealing traps. The coon is not afraid of an uncovered trap unless it has been caught before, but it is always best to make the surroundings look natural. Old unused cow or deer trails are often followed by 'coon and a trap covered in a narrow part will often make a catch.

Flesh baits are used for 'coon with varied success. A chicken or a piece of meat hung up near a 'coon run and a trap set near is considered a fair set, if it does not attract a striped "kitty." A small fish tied to the pan of a trap and placed under water along a stream will cause the downfall of some 'coon. Some use a fish made of bright tin, and others paint the pan of the trap white. Some make cubby-pens and bait with dried herring, fishheads, or eels. A few drops of anise oil is often used on the bait as a lure.

As mentioned before, the 'coon is very fond of berries. Nearly every swamp has varieties of wild berries that do not ripen until fall, or when the frosts come. If the trapper knows the locations of these berry patches, he is in position to take off a few pelts, for invariably, trails can be located leading from the food to the dens. If a stump or hummock is close by these feeding grounds, the 'coon will break off a bunch of berries and climb on the stump or hummock to eat them. A trap concealed here will often make a catch.

'Coons that live in the great wilderness sections are hard to locate, due to the fact that there are many available places for them to live. But no matter how far back in the woods they are located, they will always seek the ponds and streams when in need of food. To know what any fur-bearer eats is the next thing to learning its location.

A rail fence that is in proximity to a 'coon section is sure to be traveled more or less by these animals, and a trap placed firmly on the top rail is in good position to secure a "catch." When wandering around among swamps and woodlots, the 'coon climbs on every log that comes in line with its travels, and walks on it as far as possible. Chop out a space large enough to cause the trap to be level, and a snarling ringtail will await you on the next trip.

The raccoon will often climb on top of muskrat houses. This applies particularly to swampy sections, and to 'rat houses that have been built during extremely wet weather, which leaves them on comparatively dry land when the waters lower, or at normal periods. If a 'coon is wading about through water and catches a frog, fish, or clam, he will invariably climb to the top of a 'rat house if any is in the vicinity. I know of no easier place to conceal a trap than on the top of a muskrat house, and such sets will often take mink as well as 'coon. I have even known foxes to be taken on the top of 'rat houses, especially after the ice is thick enough to carry this animal.

'Coon skins are graded as large, medium and small. To be prime the pelt side should show no bluish tint, but should be nearly white or with a pinkish shade. The color makes a difference in the price of the fur, the darker shades commanding the most money. The northern is of course more valuable than those of the South, but the South has more 'coon and here is about the only part of the United States that trappers exist by trapping for this animal almost altogether.

The skin should be ripped down the under part of the body, which is the method known as "open," then trim the points until it is square.

# CHAPTER XV

## "CATS"

WHAT trapper has none of the feline family on his trapping grounds, with house cats, bob-cats, wild cats, lynx cats, lynx, cougar, bay cats, gone-wild cats, catamounts, panther, lions, and a dozen others. Of course many of those mentioned are the same thing in different localities.

### HAUNTS AND HABITS

All cats excepting house cats are citizens of the wilds. The habits are very much alike. They gain their food which consists of flesh, by stealth. They seek the high rocky ridges and bluffs, where they can gaze down and watch for a chance to spring upon some unsuspecting prey. They are tireless wanderers, traveling many miles in a single night.

The cougar is the largest and most ferocious of the American cat family. Terrible tales have been told of encounters on our frontier, with this animal. When traveling about at night, they occasionally emit a weird cry, which drives terror into the hearts of those not familiar with this nocturnal prowler. There are no doubt authentic accounts of attacks on humans by the cougar, but they are considered quite harmless by those who know their habits. They will, however, attack and quickly kill even a large deer, and they have been known to kill colts, heifers and many sheep, in the way of domesticated animals.

A trapper while trailing down a mountain lion, found the carcasses of nine head of cattle it had killed. This of course extended over a considerable length of time. For this reason, predatory animal hunters and trappers are employed by the Government who spend all their time exterminating them. No large amount has been brought in during any single year. The writer is not in accord with trying to exterminate any of the wood's creatures. Nature balanced up the animals, one preying on the other and keeping things equal. Take away one kind and dire results may follow. Once a certain section of the country went into the raising of waterfowl. In the spring when the young were about, a few were taken by skunks. The owners swore to clean out these obnoxious creatures, and accordingly went after them with guns, poison and traps. The drive was successful and not one was left. "Surely our ducklings will be safe now," they said. In a few years they noticed that turtles were getting more plentiful and not only the young ducks but the old ones were being taken and large flocks were rapidly depleted. Then they called a meeting, and they tried to figure out the reason for the plentifulness of the turtles. There was one person at the meeting that had once followed the vocation of trapping, and he informed them that the skunks that they had exterminated were the natural enemy of the turtle, seeking out the eggs and devouring thousands of them. The little pole-cat would have been welcomed back to this part of the world.

It may or may not be a fact that in some areas where the cougars have been killed off, that the deer

AN UNUSUAL PHOTOGRAPH OF TWO LYNX MANICURING THEIR CLAWS

became so plentiful that they ran out of food and starvation threatened the entire herd.

The largest cat of the East is known as the panther, or catamount, which is really a lynx. They are very scarce in the States, only a few being seen each year. The skins of no cats are valuable, and they are trapped mostly as a sideline. The Canadian lynx probably brings more money into the trapper's pockets than any other.

The smaller cats live much in thick swamps, feeding on rabbits, grouse, and other small denizens of this domain. They den in hollow trees, or adjacent rocky caves or crevices. Around the den will be found bones of the past victims. Some people think it terrible that one animal was made to devour some other, but "we are not to be the judge," and "what is, is right."

The smallest of the real cat family is the house cat, and few trappers are interested in knowing how to trap them successfully, but rather how to keep them from poking their feet into traps set for more valuable fur-bearers. Many a farmland trapper has been ordered from good territory, just because he mutilated the foot of the owner's pussy. However, no more ruthless game murderer roams the fields than the house cat, and the laws of the State of New York, protect and advise any person to kill every cat that is found hunting birds or other game, and any house cat that is roaming about back lots or woodlands is there for no good purpose. Where house cats are plentiful and one wishes to avoid catching them, I advise that bait be emitted when making a set.

Lynx trapping is followed to a great extent in

some sections of Canada. The Canadian lynx live off the millions of rabbits that inhabit the great swamps. Nature arranged that when rabbits got too plentiful, due to their extreme prolificness that they would contract a disease peculiar to their species, and die off until only a few breeders were left. The most of them die in thick, impenetrable places which is their natural haunt, and therefore are not seen lying about in large quantities, thus the Northern trapper usually believes that the rabbits migrate. In closely settled communities where hiding places are not easily available, I have seen hundreds of dead rabbits in one day after the disease attacked them. When the rabbits become scarce the trapper need not look for many lynx, for it is the food supply that regulates the amount of fur-bearers even more than trapping.

### SETS

Bait sets are nearly always used for every species of "cats." The trail set is of little use unless in paths leading to food, for a cat can never be depended on to do the same thing more than once. Birds are used extensively by trappers for bait, but any kind of flesh will answer. The bait pen is not used as much as for other fur-bearers, but rather the bait is hung up and the trap placed underneath in true schoolboy trapper fashion. I have known cat trappers to use common catnip for a lure and in some sections this works satisfactorily. A chance set is made by placing a trap at the edge of a rocky precipitous bluff where the animals like to prowl as stated before. The catching of pests in traps set for "cats" is the worst feature of this kind of trap-

A CAMP USED EXTENSIVELY BY TRAPPERS AND HUNTERS—ADIRONDACKS

ping. There is but little use in setting a trap in or close to a rabbit trail, although the animals run these trails considerably.

Bob-cats are often taken in sets made for foxes or other animals. I spent a half hour one day making a gang set for a fox at the partly devoured carcass of a deer. It was in the Adirondack country, and adjacent to the Seward range. The deer had probably been wounded and roamed back in that section to die. There were many fox tracks about, and as I concealed the traps by brushing light snow over them with a bough from an evergreen, I could almost see the shining red of a fox pelt that would be awaiting me on my next trip. In three days I was back over that line, and sure enough I caught the glimpse of a movement, but the golden color was absent and a two dollar bob-cat was found tangled in the traps. I never kick, however, when any furbearer visits my sets. As I killed the "cat," I thought of the hundreds of grouse and other things that owed me their life by ridding their community of this demon.

If a fallen tree can be located which lies across a ravine, a piece of flesh bait should be placed in the middle and traps concealed at each end. Or a chip can be cut from the tree and the traps set on the top. This is a good set for others than the cat family as well.

Pieces of bait thrown back in rocky caverns and under shelving rocks and traps placed near by are quite sure to land one of the cat family, if any are about.

Prospecting for "cats" is difficult work for any but a professional. They move about so stealthily that few signs are left to identify them. In sandy tracts, one can often locate their tracks, but in rocky regions, only a few claw marks are left, unless it is partly devoured victims of their sagacity.

Even the cougar is easily held in a trap, and a common number one trap will often hold a bob-cat for days. They claw about considerable, but will not chew their foot nor twist out. They are all hard to kill, and a bullet is the easiest and proper method of accomplishing it.

The animals should be skinned "cased," and stretched according to size on thin stretchers.

## CHAPTER XVI

## THE MARTEN

### HABITAT AND CHARACTERISTICS

FAR back among the silences of the green timber forest, dwells the quick-moving marten. Only a few states in the Union now have marten in plentifulness worthy of trapping. Washington, Oregon, California, New York, Idaho, Michigan, and Maine harbor the bulk of the marten in the United States, while almost every province in Canada has at least a few, and only in the wildest, most inaccessible parts of the States and Provinces mentioned are they to be found.

The marten like the rest of the weasel family, preys on its woods companion, and satisfies its voracious appetite by devouring those that are too weak to withstand the terrific onslaught of this terrible fighter. Being nimble of foot and as much at home in a tree as on the ground, its natural prey seems to be the red squirrel, but a rabbit or grouse is never to be passed up. The natural range of the marten is the high mountain regions, yet they visit swamps and lowlands at times. As the local food becomes depleted, all the marten in a section will migrate to new localities. Often a trapper that has seen no marten sign in his territory for years, suddenly finds these animals apparently plentiful along his trapline, and a welcome surprise it is. Some years ago, many trappers specialized in marten

A SIMPLE MARTEN SET

trapping, but today I do not believe there are one hundred marten specialists in America. If the green timber was removed at the rate it has been going the past ten years, for ten years more, the marten would be a thing of the past, for this shy dweller of the wilds never adapts himself to civilization, like many other fur-bearers have done. Fortunately, the United States Government as well as the various states have now decided on conserving the forests and even reforesting, so the future of the marten is now more hopeful.

### TRAPPING METHODS

Marten are known as an easy animal to trap, yet like every other fur-bearer, there are trappers who can make good money at the game when others would starve. Bait sets are practically the only kind made, and they may be either of the ground or tree variety. The hollow snag set is conceded the best. Locate a hollow snag in good marten country and if there is not a hole near the bottom, chop one through to the inside. Here will be found plenty of dry rotted wood; a natural covering for the trap. It is not necessary to conceal a marten trap with a covering, but if there are fisher in the region and the trap is powerful enough to hold one it is advisable to use a light, dry covering like the one previously mentioned. After the trap which may be a number 1 if the marten is the only animal sought is placed in position, a flesh bait must be put in a position so that the marten will have to pass over the trap to reach the bait. The flesh of the deer, moose, or even rabbit or porcupine will work.

A TRAP SET AT A BAIT PEN. A ROOF OF EVERGREEN BOUGHS MUST BE ADDED FOR DEEP SNOW TRAPPING

A method recommended by a British Columbia trapper is called the big cedar set. Locate a cedar that has been climbed much by squirrels and martens. This can be done by noting the numerous claw-marks of each animal. Apparently the marten climb these trees in pursuit of squirrels. The trap should be set at the bottom and bait may be hung up on the tree.

Sometimes a piece of bait is hung about ten feet up on a tree, and then a pole leaned against the tree and a trap placed in a notch made with an axe, about one-half way up.

A common set is to drive two pins into a soft tree which makes a shelf for a trap. Hardwood pins should be used. A piece of flesh bait is hung about eighteen inches above the trap.

Tree sets are not bothered by mice and other rodents, and sets made in hollow trees are not located by eagles, owls, or "devils."

In the deep snow country a trapper must rely on tree sets or else roof his sets with evergreen boughs, bark or other material.

If no hollow tree or natural bait pen is available one should build a "cubby-pen" of slabs or heavy bark. This should be made in a V shape and the bait placed in the pointed end. A spring-pole can be used to an advantage at this kind of a set. This is made by bending down a sapling and fastening it in a notch so that the trapped animal will release it during its struggles to escape, and be lifted into the air, where it will be safe from wandering flesh eaters. An animal that is kept in a dry manner and out of the damp snow will not hair-slip easily.

HOLLOW TREE SETS ARE USED FOR MARTEN AND OTHER FUR BEARERS

Where snow is not deep, a pole can be leaned against a large tree and then a piece of flesh hung from the pole about one-half way up. It should be tied with string or moose-wood bark so that it will hang down within three feet of the ground. A trap should then be placed on the ground and a little to one side of the bait. Some marten trappers add a little oil of anise for a lure.

To prevent marten traps from freezing down, some trappers place the traps on a slab of cedar or other bark. This is a good method and one used extensively in Canada.

An experienced marten trapper can spot a natural set the moment he sees it. Here in the Adirondack Mountains, we look for jutting points that partially connect two mountain ranges. A bait set at one of these points will often take a dozen martens or sable as they are commonly known in the 'Dacks in one season. Old lumber roads seem to be favorite runways of marten after they have been abandoned for many years. I once found a regular path of marten in the Indian Pass region, on a grown-up lumber "tote" road. I stuck up a piece of bait on a half dozen trees adjacent to this road and set traps underneath and I picked off a half dozen in as many nights.

Around animal killings are favorite places to look for marten sign. The prospective trapper will know of every deer or other paunch left in his territory with good sets in view at a later period. Old time trappers shot big game animals in the deep forest for no other purpose than to coax up marten, fisher, lynx, and fox. Sometimes a deer will die of wounds or for other reasons. I never found one of these in marten country that did not have tracks around it, and once they get to feeding, the trapper can count on their return, unless some other trapper lands him first, and competition is not apt to be brisk in the regions inhabited by marten.

The marten makes its den in trees or rocky crevices. A few persons have undertaken to raise them in captivity, and part of these have succeeded. During the months of May and June one can sometimes locate the young and capture them, but usually the wild stock is secured by catching in box traps or steel traps with the jaws wound to prevent leg breakage.

Tracks of the marten are like his smaller brothers the mink and weasel, excepting on a larger scale. The animal does not hibernate to any great extent, and in the dead of winter when nothing else is available to the wilderness trapper, but weasels, fox, and lynx, the marten sets should be kept in good working condition.

A marten trapper seldom can handle a line of more than fifty traps to advantage.

The fur of the marten is graded mainly as to color, the darker shades commanding the top price. The fur is used to substitute the more valuable Russian sable.

## CHAPTER XVII

## THE WEASEL

### HAUNTS AND HABITS

THE weasel is the smallest of its family, scorned by the trapper of a few years ago, and as eagerly sought at the present time. It is the most blood-thirsty of the whole species, and kills even after its voracious appetite is satiated, just for the love of killing. Unlucky is the brood of grouse that is located by this fiend in animal form. Very often the skunk, fox, or others of the furry denizens are blamed for misdeeds committed by this sneaky individual.

The weasel is found in almost every section of United States and Canada. It makes its home in wilderness and settlement localities, apparently having no preference. It dens in hollow logs, stumps, or trees. The young which consist of any amount up to ten, arrive about May in the North, and often there is another litter in late summer. The weasel is the greatest natural enemy of the field mouse, and I have found more than a dozen, killed and stored away in the den. Wherever there are plenty of mice is a good place to look for weasels. They hang around old buildings just to hunt these rodents. They kill many rabbits also, and are only second to that red renegade, the fox, in depleting the ranks of this trapline pest. The weasel apparently likes cold weather and stirs about more at this time than at any other. For this reason it can be trapped when few other furry citizens are stirring. It runs long distances in a night and often covers the same territory twice or more. For this reason it is about impossible to track one of these slick beauties to a den. It changes its color from a deep brown in summer to a pure white in winter. This is Nature's way of protecting it, for its color harmonizes with the surroundings at any time of year. Up until a few years ago, only the pure white skins had any value, but at the present time there is but little difference in the value. The graybacks, however, which is a mixture of both colors and which are procured when the color is changing, has but little value commercially. The weasel moves about in the daytime nearly as much as at night. The largest one I ever killed, I shot in daylight. I was trapping for skunk, and I caught a cotton-tail rabbit in a den. When I arrived at the set, I noted that something was eating from the carcass of the rabbit. In fact it was more than one-half gone. I was about to remove it from the trap, when a weasel poked its head out of the hole and quickly snatched a bite from the carcass. I yanked my Colt auto from the holster and tried to get a shot, but the animal was now out of sight. In a moment it came out again and I stood quiet until it began to eat. Then I fired. I pulled about two feet of this animal out of the den before I came to the tip of its tail. Once in camp at Cold River in the Adirondacks, I noticed fresh weasel tracks around the front of the log cabin. I had some fresh killed venison in camp, and I placed a piece about five rods out. In a few moments I looked out and the little fur-bearer was smelling at the flesh. The skin was white and I did not wish to ruin it by shooting, so I took out a trap, and when I approached, it ran under the wood-pile. I set the trap and watched from the window. In about ten minutes it came out and went directly to the bait. It fed for a while before it stepped on the pan of the trap. Later I caught two more at this same bait. This was the easiest trapping I ever did, but I had a partner that was tracking a mink as it appeared to be going in the same direction he was toward an old camp where he intended staying all night. It continued in the same direction and when the trapper arrived at the cabin, he was surprised to find that the animal had gone under the floor. He placed a trap at the hole, and had the mink on the following morning.

The weasel jumps with two feet in a place, that is, side by side. The distance will vary according to the size of the animal, but will average two and one half feet of a jump. It emits a yellow scent when aroused, which when it gets on the pure white fur causes it to grade "stained," as no chemical has yet been discovered that will entirely remove this.

For its size, the weasel is the hardest animal to kill that exists. The head is small and a person can hardly hit it with a club. It can make a loud squealing noise, and often I have heard them make this noise at night. If one is in a trap, and a person goes near enough, he is quite apt to get a fierce bite on the leg. Usually the trap is large enough that it grips around the body, thus obviating the necessity of killing the animal. A number 1 trap will hold a weasel, but it is so small that when the

BAITED WEASEL SET

(174)

animal winds itself about the trap, it is impossible to remove it if the weather is cold enough to freeze it in this position. Therefore the number 1 or 1½ is about right for weasel.

Swamps and lowlands are the natural haunts of the weasel, for here is found the kind of home it prefers, but when running at night it will visit any kind of territory. Stone walls, brush-heaps, corn-shocks, and under bridges are favorite haunts.

Very few states protect the weasel and a few offer a bounty for its extermination, but even with all their faults, they add a good bit of coin to the trapper's pocket in a time when he usually needs it badly.

I have known a few professional weasel trappers that trapped for no other fur-bearer. With prices ranging up to two or more dollars, one can make good money, for it is not uncommon for a live weasel trapper in a good section to procure twenty in a day.

Bait sets are the only kind worth considering for the weasel. Nearly any kind of flesh can be used, but it should be fresh and bloody to work good as a call. A fresh killed rabbit is the best bait I know of, and if bait is scarce it may be cut in two pieces. If a weasel is very hungry it will eat stale bait, otherwise it will pass it up. If one of these little fur-bearers once locates a piece of bait that it likes, it will hang around that vicinity as long as there is a particle left. The most trouble in trapping weasel is that being such a light weight animal, it will often pass over a trap and fail to spring it. To correct this, the trapper files the "dog" until the lightest weasel will cause the trap to function. Occasionally a mouse or mole will be found in the trap, but this is unavoidable. A few mice thrown down beside the bait will be found to improve the set. If the bait is not well hidden from the sharp eyes of the Canadian jay, known in the land of big sticks as the "whisky-jack," they will molest the set and be found awaiting the trapper.

Often one can find a natural bait pen when preparing a set for weasel, but if none is located, and weasel tracks are to be seen, a pen must be built. Flat pieces of bark make fine "cubby" pens. Pieces of flat stone or slabs of wood are equally good. Ends of hollow logs, holes under stumps or rocks, or spaces in snags, are natural bait pens. When building a pen, make it in the shape of a V and place the bait in the pointed end. The trap should be placed at the front. The professional usually waits until he finds a natural set. He makes sure that the spot will not be reached by snow and sleet, and he throws down a piece of bait and sets a trap beside it. The weasel shows no fear of a steel trap, and will climb on top of one to get to the meat. They can smell fresh blood for long distances. One day in the fall I was hunting deer in the Adirondack Mountains. There was snow on the ground, and I followed the tracks of a big buck over a mountain range and down into a valley. In the valley was a dense growth of balsam and fir, and I suspected the animal would be laying up out of the storm and cold at this point. I advanced cautiously, making no sound with deer skin pacs. Suddenly I saw the animal crouched under an evergreen. He saw me at the same moment and jumped. There was a tiny clearing ahead and I knocked the big fellow down at this point.

Running up hastily, I drew my hunting knife and severed the main artery of his neck. The blood spurted into the air. Even before the deer quit kicking, I heard a terrible squealing, and looking in the direction from whence the noise came, could see nothing. But I had heard this sound before and I looked close. Yes, there it was, a large blood-thirsty weasel squealing defiance at me, and threatening to come and get some of the fresh blood, even with me close by.

I watched him for some time but he did not venture nearer than twenty feet, but all the time he screeched and threatened. He was so near the color of the snow that at times I could only distinguish the black tip of its tail. Finally I got a bead with my 22 belt gun and I added a pelt to my collection. Wondering how far it had smelled the blood, I followed the tiny track backward. One-eighth of a mile away I found where he had come out of a hollow stump and no fresh tracks showed when it came there. Evidently the animal had been sleeping in the den, when the odor of fresh blood was wafted his way. He awoke immediately and took a straight line to the spot where I first saw him.

If a weasel can smell bait for an eighth of a mile, it is no wonder that a good trapper using plenty of bloody flesh and making many sets can make good money trapping this fur-bearer alone. And every weasel that is caught saves the life of many dozen grouse, song birds, rabbits, squirrels, etc. To say nothing of the winning of the gratitude of every farmer and poultry raiser in your locality.

Embryo trappers often mistake the tracks of a large weasel for that of a small mink. Not that the

TRAPPED WEASEL

tracks look much alike when they are seen together, but rather because the habits are somewhat alike. The weasel always leaves but two imprints close together, while the mink either walks or leaves the print of every foot in proximity.

This is part of the knack of trapping. To know the footprints of an animal is one thing, and to be able to distinguish between two animal tracks that appear similar is another.

The professional weasel trapper puts out his bait when the animal is unprime and in the grayback class. Then later he puts out his traps and reaps a rich harvest very quickly.

There are certain times in winter that but few other fur-bearers roam, but if one is out looking for weasel sign, he will invariably locate a frozen out 'rat or some other animal that has been obliged to move.

Few other animals will molest the weasel in your trap. In a few instances, I have known other weasels to chew up the trapped victim. This however is not the rule. Field mice will chew tiny holes in the pelt if the animal is not removed from the trap in a reasonable length of time.

Occasionally I have caught weasel in blind sets. If a weasel is traveling a route regular, like many other fur-bearers, he will go under the same stumps and visit the same stone piles, and will usually enter at the same place. If a person does not have any bait with him, and wishes to catch the animal, he can do so by placing a trap or two at some of these entrances.

Under old hay and straw stacks are favorable spots to look for weasel and to make sets. Usually there are spaces under the edge of these stacks that can be utilized as shelter by different fur-bearers. Innumerable mice live under stacks, and this is an inducement for the weasel to stop and search about. A piece of flesh bait placed in one of these spaces and a trap set at the side will take every one of these animals that roams the vicinity. A muskrat carcass makes good bait for the weasel, and the 'rat trapper can often pick up a little loose change by dropping down the carcasses in a sheltered spot and placing a trap close by.

I have used "dead shot" rat traps for weasel with success. These are the type of trap that has two coiled springs and a stiff wire that strikes the ordinary barn rat a wallop hard enough to kill it, when the bait is pulled. The tree trap works on the same principle and will catch weasels, but generally speaking the regular type of plain jaw steel trap should be used. A professional weasel trapper in a good territory should be able to handle two hundred traps to advantage.

Weasel skins are graded as to size and quality as well as color. The skin is tender and extreme care must be taken while skinning. The tail-bone should be removed and the skin which must be cased, may then be stretched on a narrow thin board.

## CHAPTER XVIII

### FISHER AND WOLVERINE

"Set less traps, but set more of them."—
OLD TRAPPER.

#### HAUNTS AND HABITS

THE fisher and wolverine are so closely allied in their range and habits, that I will class them together. Few trappers make a business of trapping either one due to their scarceness, but pursue them as a side line in connection with other trapping. Both make their home in the wildest, and most mountainous sections of the United States, Canada and Alaska.

The fisher cat, known in some regions as the "pekan," resembles the common mink somewhat, excepting that it is much larger, and will run about three feet from tip to tip. In color they vary from a light brown to a black, and sometimes contain a sprinkling of white hairs, giving them a silver effect.

The wolverine is much larger, sometimes reaching the hundred pound mark. In color this furbearer runs from brown to black, with a sort of stripe running along the sides of the body. This stripe coupled with the fact that the body is shaped like that of the bear, gives it the name of "skunk-bear." It is also known in the extreme north as "Injun Devil," and is supposed by Indians to be possessed with a bad spirit.

The food of both animals consists of any kind of flesh that they can locate. It matters not whether they kill it themselves or find the "kill" of some other prowler. Either one will not hesitate to attack a lynx or almost any other woods denizen, regardless of size, if there is food to dispute, and invariably they come out the victor. The quill pig seems to be the natural food of the pekan, and around the dens of these animals are favorable places to look for signs of fisher. Unlike the lynx, the fisher knows that he must avoid eating the quills, and so he begins at the neck and skins out the "pig" leaving the skin intact, except for the first opening.

The fisher has a regular route which he covers in from one to three weeks, and he will have regular crossings where he goes from one mountain range to another. If a fisher's track is once located, you may be sure that he will come back, and especially if one can locate where he has dined from a deer or other carcass. Some naturalists claim that a fisher will kill a deer, but this is doubtful, unless it be a small fawn, or a deer weak from hunger. They can climb a tree easily, and will go up after a porky or other prospects of a feed.

Both animals are members of the weasel or mustela family, and emit a disagreeable odor when molested. The wolverine is the largest of the species.

The track of the fisher is not unlike that of a large marten, especially when loping. When walking, the tracks sometimes resemble those of a small fox. The wolverine's track is large and rather sprawling.

Wolverine and sometimes fisher will follow a trapline and eat or chew up every trapped animal.

ON THE TRAPLINE IN WINTER

This is one reason that trappers operating in their environments, invariably use the spring or balance pole to lift the catch out of reach, and even then they may climb. Many stories have been written of trappers being obliged to vacate their chosen grounds, because of the havoc created by a wolverine. A good backwoods trapper however, will make short work of one of these fur-bearers that molest his catches.

### TRAPPING METHODS

Bait sets are used almost altogether for both animals. For fisher, the trapper will do well to use porcupine flesh, although any meat will do. A large bait will hold odor better than a small one. As most fisher trapping is done amid deep snows, one must be constantly placing his traps where the storms cannot reach. In the end of a hollow log, or under shelving rocks are good locations for sets. The bait should be placed at the back, and the trap concealed at the front. Fisher are more or less elusive, and all human odors should be eliminated as much as possible on the trap and bait, and one should avoid leaving unnecessary signs around the set. Trappers working the same fisher section for years will usually have many bait or cubby pens built. I do not recommend the building of fresh pens for fisher sets, but prefer the natural pens when one is trapping new territory. Some fisher trappers draw a beaver tail from one set to another, claiming that a fisher will follow this trail. Others drag a piece of flesh of any kind for ten rods on either side of the set. Old fisher trappers prefer sets made near the summits of mountain ranges, claiming that the animals run these more than other places. The fisher, contrary to name, does no fishing, and visits the streams less than any other fur-bearer.

Around deep paunches or any carcass left in the woods, is the place to make sets and look for signs. This applies to nearly all the wilderness roamers. A number two trap of the best make is none too powerful for fisher, for they fight to the very last, and often leg themselves, unless the trapper used a spring pole or a trap made with a provision for preventing gnawing. When arriving at a set where there is a "trapped" fisher, one should not be careless and approach too closely, for they will sometimes jump with lightning quickness and fasten their teeth in the leg or any part of the body they can reach, and a bite from any trapped animal in a wilderness section is apt to end with dire results. Should one be bitten at any time, he should apply iodine quickly as a germ killer and antiseptic.

In the Adirondack country, fisher have been on the increase for some years. I know of some trappers that catch as many as ten in one season, in connections with other furs. Choice, dark fisher skins sometimes sell as high as $100, but this is very rare, and more often they run from $35 to $50. I have seen tracks of a half dozen different fisher in one day. Occasionally, they may be tracked in, but often one will be obliged to camp on the trail. When located, they will be found in hollow snags, logs, or stumps. A slight smoke will drive a fisher out of a den very quickly, and the smoke guns sold by fur houses are ideal for this purpose.

Wolverine have a reputation of being uncanny, elusive. This has been gained by many stories that have been written and circulated by swivel chair

A TRAPPER'S LINE CAMP IN THE ROCKY MOUNTAINS

nature writers. I have known them to be taken in an uncovered, fully exposed trap, and certainly, any trapper that can trap a fox or otter, can catch a wolverine. One of the best methods is to "double cross 'em." This is accomplished by making a common marten set with exposed trap, and then conceal a powerful number four close by. When the gormandish "devil" tries to rob your bait pen, he finds himself tangled with the "iron dog." Or a large bait house may be erected which the animal can enter, and bait placed in the back and a small, uncovered trap located inside. Then a large trap must be set at the entrance. When the snow is thawing and freezing, the large trap should be placed inside and the small one omitted. A large bird makes good wolverine bait.

A wolverine has been known to visit a trapper's camp when he is absent and eat or otherwise destroy the most of his food. If one can locate a trail which is used regularly, a trap concealed will take the oldest and wisest.

Beaver castor, anise oil and fish oil, are used as a lure for fisher and wolverine, although only a few ever care to lure the latter to their trapping territory.

Fisher farming is now carried on to a considerable extent. There are more than one dozen fur farms in New York state that raise these animals in captivity. Some states do not have any protection on fisher and trappers keep out box traps all summer, knowing that wild stock will be in good demand for propagation purposes. The fisher does not tame readily, but will eat almost anything and is very rugged.

The skins should be removed as for "cased," and a long and comparatively narrow stretcher should be used. A good type is the adjustable kind, made in three pieces, with a wedge-shaped part for the middle. The skin is easily removed from this stretcher by withdrawing the wedge. This kind of stretcher is good for any long animal.

The wolverine like all other animals of its shape, is usually skinned "open." All flesh should be removed.

The fisher fur is graded as to size and color, the darkest and silkiest skins commanding the most money. The wolverine is graded as to size and quality of fur.

GREEN TIMBER, THE HAUNT OF FISHER, MARTEN, AND LYNX

## CHAPTER XIX

### THE ELUSIVE WOLF

"Set your traps where the animal is going to go."—KID TRAPPER.

#### HAUNTS AND HABITS

THE American wolf is found in the most heavily timbered sections of the United States and Canada, while the coyote being of a smaller species is found on the plains and in the brush country. Wolves were once very plentiful in the eastern part of the states, but are now found in very limited numbers. A cousin to the dog; he is considered by many as the wisest of the species or even of the whole furry tribe. The wolf has been a great detriment to sheep raising, and in many states, bounties are offered all the year round. Expert wolfers are also hired by the Government, who use poison, and dig the puppies from their dens. We of the trapline hate to be obliged to allow such happenings, but the other fellow looks at the thing from a different viewpoint.

Much discussion has been going on for some time regarding whether wolves attack humans; some asserting that they are great cowards and never attack persons, and others speaking with the same assuredness, state that many individuals have met their fates during encounters with wolf packs. The fact is that both are probably right as regards their sections. Wolves in sections where natural food is plentiful never attacks humans, but animals on the verge of starvation and in large numbers will attack anything. I knew of a pack of wild dogs that roamed the Adirondack region at one time, and they did not hesitate to attack persons until they were exterminated by the aid of a rifle. I have even known of hundreds of rats to attack persons who were trying to exterminate them. This happened in underground passages under New York City. Ordinarily, however, the wolf is not to be considered dangerous, and the trapper is only too glad to get sight of one when out in the woods, especially if the trusty rifle is along.

The coyote is nearly like a large fox in size, and the habits are very much alike, excepting the coyote lives in dens more. They are never brave and a small dog will chase one. I spent some time in a sction of western Canada at one time, and there was a coyote that had a den up in a run back of the dwelling where I was staying. We had a cur dog at the place and every evening this dog would go out and seek that coyote. Seemingly it would be hanging around back of the buildings for the dog would soon locate it. Then would begin a chase which lasted until the coyote gained his natural haunts. Then I never knew whether the coyote turned and drove the dog back or not, but anyway the dog would soon come back on the run with the coyote a few rods behind. Then when the dog got near the buildings, he became brave again and turned on the little wolf which showed that it lacked courage by wheeling and racing back. Sometimes this continued until a half dozen trips were made.

The wolf of today is probably much larger to take in traps or by poisoning than the wolf of a hundred years ago. Time and experience has caused the wolves to develop a more thoroughly educated strain in order to subsist with the more plentiful amount of trappers, the modern methods of trapping and poisoning, and the better firearms. All the fur-bearers have adapted themselves in the same way. Every trapper knows that the same trapping methods will not work in the same section year after year, and there is no doubt that the elusive animals learn in time to associate the odor of man with danger when connected with the same circumstances. Whether an animal learns from seeing other animals in traps is doubtful, yet possible.

The food of the wolf consists of almost any other species of animal that he can kill, and when combined in packs, they often attack and kill animals as large as deer. They will however, feed off any carcass that is lying near their lines of travel. Calves and even yearling heifers have been slain by packs of wolves. They vary in color from the dark gray of the North to the much lighter shades of the central and southern sections.

Individuality must be considered more in wolf trapping than in the taking of any other fur-bearer. A set that would take one wolf would not do for another. By observing tracks, the trapper can often devise sets for the particular animal he is seeking.

## TRAPPING METHODS

In placing out a line of traps for wolves the trapper must be continually making his sets with the one thought in view: the elimination of human odor.

TRAPPED COYOTE

Like the fox and other elusive dwellers of the wilds, the wolf is easier taken in water sets, especially by the amateur, for a trap under water is surely free of odor. The wolf however, like the rest of the dog family, is quite averse to placing his "tootsies" in water. Occasionally, wolves and coyotes will have crossing places in shallow streams, and here is the place to take the oldest and shyest. The traps with the fastenings must be completely under water, and I advise that a half dozen traps be used, for a wolf will not take any unnecessary steps when crossing a stream, and it is easy to miss one.

The No. 4 trap is considered about right for wolves, and there is a trap known as the "Ranger," that is a great favorite with old wolfers. The method of fastening known as a "dead man" to the western trapper is commonly used. This simply implies that the clog is buried in the earth or snow. A pronged drag may also be used, but on sections of the plains where there is little to hold a drag it is hardly advisable to use one.

The stink scent is used in wolf trapping about the same as for fox. Cat-flesh, mice, and hoof-parings are allowed to rot, and then skunk essence, fish oil, and beaver castor is added. Sex scent is made from the urine and matrix of the female dog, fox, or wolf when in season, and is useful mainly during the mating season.

Trail sets are made much in the same manner as described for trapping the fox. A coyote method is to fell a tree over a stock trail. This will turn the stock so they will be obliged to go around, and should be done in summer. The coyote will stick to the old trail and go under the tree. Then when the time comes, and preferably during a rainstorm, make an excavation in the trail and place in the trap, covering it carefully, first with soft material like leaves, and then dirt. When visiting this set or any other set for the elusive animals, never go closer than is absolutely necessary to ascertain whether a catch has been made or not. Many coyote trappers look at their traps from a horse's back, which is the best known method. A good pair of field glasses will enable the trapper to keep farther back.

Trappers who depend on scent, make sets for both wolves and coyotes by placing a small amount on a stick or bush close to a run and setting a trap on each side. Partly rotted flesh may be buried and a trap covered on the top. This will take any wolf that tries to dig up the bait. Only when natural foods are scarce are flesh baits very valuable, and where snowshoe rabbits and other small animals are plentiful, one must depend on blind setting to a great extent. Some trappers use short chains on their wolf traps or else fasten closely so that the animal will not be able to run and jump, thus being liable to get free.

Snow trapping for wolves is usually done by placing a bait in a likely place and setting traps around it during a snowstorm, or else make the set in an open place and put the traps in excavations in the snow, where the wind will quickly drift snow over them. Drifted snow is harder than snow that has fallen naturally however, and I heartily advise the former method. Some trappers make sets at all the baits in his section late in the fall and take a chance on a proper snowfall before the animals have time to familiarize themselves with the set. I have known wolves at these times to get caught in an uncovered trap after the human odors had vanished, proving once more that the animal's nose is the key to his brain and not his eyes.

Poisoning seems to be the favorite method of taking wolves and coyotes by the majority of wolfers. I do not recommend the use of poison for any fur-bearer, mainly because it is liable to kill at any time whether the fur is prime or not, and because other animals often eat it. Many wolves take poison and are snowed under and are never found.

To those who insist on using poison I will give the common method. Tiny pills are made by enclosing poison in a drop of tallow or preferably, blood. These are either dropped near bait or enclosed in pieces of flesh bait. Sometimes the tallow pills are placed on snags along the edges of lakes and ponds, where wolves frequent during the winter months.

The Government wolf trappers usually do their trapping on horseback, as wolves do not fear the odor of the horse. Arriving at a set, the trapper throws down a piece of clean canvas and stands on this when making the set. A few days after placing the traps, he returns and drops down scent near the traps. The urine of wolves, the anal glands, and the gall are used in making this scent.

The prairie dog set is also used extensively, and is made as follows: A prairie dog is killed and then fastened to a stick at the edge of a burrow so that it will appear to be going into the den. A trap is then concealed on each side of the "dog." They may be fastened by driving a stake down to the level of the ground with the trap-chain made fast to it. The end of this fastening stake should be covered with earth or grass.

Wolf traps should be covered with dry earth or other natural material. Moss or other fluffy material placed under the trap-pan will prevent the covering from interfering with the proper functioning of the trap. The trap-bed should be lined with dry leaves, pine needles or other unfreezable material during cold weather.

Some trappers carry a burlap sack when making sets and stand on this when making a set. Others cover the trap with straw or other dry material and then fire it, depending on the fire to eliminate the human odor, and the ashes to cover the trap. The well known "camp fire" set is made by adding bits of bacon or meat scraps.

Den sets are not particularly productive, yet wolves and coyotes visit old dens often, especially during late winter. Traps should not be placed in the opening or entrance, but placed near the outside, and covered carefully.

Wolf and coyotes always visit the carcasses of horses, cattle or sheep that lay near their natural habitat, and traps may be set at these places. The commonest mistake when making a carcass set is to set too many traps and place them too close to the carcass. The purpose of a carcass is not to make a set location, but to lure the animals into the vicinity. If the carcass is placed as an attractor, it should be in a brushy section where there will be sure to be trails leading to and from the bait. If not then one must look for trails. If a stump or hummock is near, the animals will climb on this to view the surrounding territory in search of enemies before going up to feed. A trap concealed at this point will be apt to make a catch.

Wolf hides should be stretched fur side out and skinned "cased."

THE AUTHOR IN FRONT OF HIS ADIRONDACK CAMP

## CHAPTER XX

### MISCELLANEOUS FUR-BEARERS

*In this chapter I will mention those animals that are but little trapped, due to scarcity, small value, and other causes.*

#### OPOSSUM

THIS fur-bearer is a native of the southern part of the United States. They feed on flesh and fruits. They seemingly do not prefer any particular kind of territory to make their home, but will thrive anywhere that the climate is warm enough and natural food plentiful. Up till a few years ago the fur was worth so little that few bothered making any efforts to catch them, excepting for food. When skunk got to the five dollar point, it was found that 'possum fur made a fair substitute when dyed, and the price of the skins of the little animal rose considerably.

The 'possum makes its home in hollow logs, stumps or in the ground. They are good climbers and will occasionally occupy a snag which has the den entrance at the top.

'Possums are hunted at night with dogs in about the same manner as the northerner hunt skunks and 'coons. After a successful hunt there is sure to be a roast and a jolly time.

In trapping for 'possum, one may use the den entrance set or the bait set. The animal does not fear a trap, and if a den can be located which appears to be occupied or being visited by the species, it is only necessary to place a trap in front and fasten it to a light log. If the animal is to remain for more than short periods in the trap, it is best to use especially constructed jaws to prevent bone breaking, chewing and twisting.

A piece of partly decayed flesh placed in the end of a hollow log and a trap set in front will take any 'possum that comes within smelling distance. Persimmon or paw-paw fruit are also used for baiting, and traps set under the trees that are bearing matured fruit will take some of the animals.

A slight blow will cause a 'possum to curl up and appear quite dead, but once you leave it, life comes back quickly and it does the disappearing act. Or if a person attempts to handle a 'possum when it is playing dead, a bitten hand may be the result.

### BADGER

This animal is about the size of a fox, but has shorter legs. It is a native of the prairie country and invariably lives in underground dens. The food consists of carrion, fruits or grains. The fur has a fair value and the hair is used for making fine brushes for artist's work.

One of the peculiar things about the badger is that it can dig faster than any other animal, and if a person attempts to dig one from his den, the animal can dig faster than the person. It has even been said that if a badger gets a fair gain on a pursuer, that it will dig itself into the ground in a few moments. They are powerful animals and it takes a good trap to hold one. The $1\frac{1}{2}$ trap is commonly used, but I consider this too small.

ON THE TRAPLINE—TREE IN DISTANCE USED AS DEN BY 'COON

Den sets are used almost exclusively for this fur-bearer. Tracks or bits of fur at the mouth of the den will tell the trapper if he may expect a catch. The trap should be well fastened or it will be missing when the pursuer visits it.

## MOLES

These tiny fur-bearers live in underground passages. The largest of the species inhabit the western states. Occasionally, the mole comes to the surface and leaves small mounds. They destroy grain by injuring the roots when burrowing underneath.

There are many types of mole traps on the market, all of the killer type. To catch them, the tunnel must be opened and the trap placed in position. A number naught steel trap of the regular type may be used if the excavation is made large enough for it to function freely. After placing the trap, a sod should be placed over the opening.

Moles should be skinned "open," and then stretched flat on boards to dry. All other fur-bearers mentioned in this chapter should be skinned "open."

## RABBITS

The fur of the wild rabbit is not valuable, but they are often trapped for bait, food, or to reduce their numbers. They feed on barks, roots, and grasses. In the woods country, all that is necessary to make a good rabbit set is to cut down a poplar or alder tree and set traps close to the limbs. In the farmlands, a bunch of clover hay will attract them for long distances.

Rabbits when moving about, follow trails and

paths are often beaten into the snow for six or more inches. A trap set in one of these trails, and a stick placed to guide one into the trap is a sure set. The cotton-tail rabbit like the jack, lives in dens in the earth or under shocks of grain and brush piles. Traps set around these dens will take many rabbits.

The flesh of the rabbit is liked by many, and as it is about the only game that can be bought and sold in every section without fear of getting mixed up with the game laws, thousands are sold in New York City alone each year. A rabbit trapper can make a fair profit pursuing these animals alone. When catching for food purposes, it is advisable to use a fine wire made preferably of copper for a snare. This should be looped and placed in their runs. A spring-pole is an aid to the snare and lifts the animal away from rodents that would mutilate it.

The bone in the foreleg of a rabbit is very small and breaks easily, and a high-gripping trap should be used if one is trapping with steel traps.

## WOODCHUCKS

This animal is found over an extensive area. The fur has but little commercial value, and is only quoted occasionally by some market that has an order for it. A few cities have a market for the flesh, and some states have a bounty on this animal.

They live in dens in the earth which they dig themselves and which are often appropriated by the skunk. They feed on clover and other grasses, and do considerable damage to the farmer both by this method of feeding, and by digging great excavations in the meadows. The writer as a sportsman, excuses them of this crime, just to take a pot shot at one occasionally to keep the shooting irons in condition, and give a person a little practice.

For trapping them, a $1\frac{1}{2}$ trap or a 115X should be used, and the trap set at a den entrance. When caught, they put up a strong fight as they are a husky animal, and the trap should be fastened securely. The hide of the 'chuck makes strong leather or when cut into strips in its raw state, makes good laces.

# CHAPTER XXI

### INCIDENTS ON THE TRAPLINE

"A trapper is not made in a day, but like the engineer, the carpenter, and the master mechanic, must serve his apprenticeship and work himself up from the beginning."
—DAILEY.

I STARTED trapping at an early age. Born in Saint Lawrence County, New York State, I spent my childhood exploring its rippling streams and forest silences. Young in years today, yet I have trapped for practically every American fur-bearer.

Strange things happen in the trapper's country, and being remote from newspaper districts, secrets remain so. The "code of the trapline" is "play square." Unfortunately, a few fail in this, and often with dire results. Bruce Brown was a quiet, unimposing trapper, who lived in a cabin of logs and stone, by the still waters of Elbow Pond. Many were the silky furs that he brought to market each spring—until another with a shady reputation erected a camp at Pine Pond, adjacent to Elbow. It was a free country and the latter person had a right to do this and to set traps where he wished. It was easier, however, to follow the trapline of his neighbor and pilfer his sets. One day the trapper from Elbow caught the other removing a choice mink from his trap. A fight ensued, in which the thief became worsted. Being revengeful, he planned to burn the other out. One night when everything was dry and the wind in the right direction, the fire was kindled, a tiny flame that soon spread to a conflagration, filled the forest creatures with awe, and they ran blindly, some away from the fire and some directly into it. The fur thief laughed with glee as the flames threatened to engulf his neighbor. Circling about he tried to gain a more favorable location, where he might watch the other perish. Unknown to the other, Old Bruce had that day placed a bear trap where a bear had been rooting about among some rotted logs. The thief and would-be murderer stepped squarely into it. Worse still, the wind quickly changed, saving the trapper and his cabin, but burning the trapped "victim of his own sins."

Another trap and fur thief met his fate in Wild Cat valley. This was a sly sneakum, as elusive as the animals of the wild. Different trappers suffered from losses, but none could catch the thief in the act. Always he sold more fur than the others, yet he never was known to buy a trap, and seldom ran a trapline extending more than a mile. One day he was found lying on the floor of his cabin—dead. There were no marks on him, yet he was a powerful man and not likely to be troubled with heart trouble or anything that would bring about his death.

Some said "lightning," but no person saw any. People had their opinions, but his death went down in the history of the Adirondacks where it happened, as an unsolved mystery.

The remains of the cabin still stands, and some say that strange sounds issue from it on certain nights. At any rate, the traplines of the valley were unmolested from that time.

### UNUSUAL CATCHES

I was trapping foxes in the sand-hills of New York. On a trail around an abrupt point, I had previously concealed two traps. On this particular morning, I heard a commotion as I arrived near the set. On coming close, I found a fox in each trap, fighting in a way that threatened to ruin the pelts of each. The traps were set within six inches of each other, and fastened to the same clog. I presume one fox had become fast about the time the other arrived, and it rushed up, either to try and aid it, or to fight it. I was a well pleased trapper.

At a particularly good skunk den, I set three traps. It was nearly dark when I arrived at the set on the following trip. In the dusk I could see two of the animals outside the den. Drawing my belt gun, I killed them, and after removing from the traps, prepared to put the set in order. The third trap was down in the den, apparently buried under the loose dirt, and it took quite a pull to remove it. The reason soon was evident, for as the trap quickly freed, a large white skunk landed fairly under my feet, and the odor "skunkibus" was being passed around freely.

At one time I was pursuing an especially elusive fisher in the Adirondack region. These animals usually came easy, once their runs were located. This one had apparently had some trapline experience himself, for he evaded my most carefully made sets with the ease of an otter on snow. Time after time I was sure that I had a set made that would

TAKING A SHOT AT GAME, ON TRAPPING STREAM ADJACENT TO THE ST. LAWRENCE

take him, and as many times I was disappointed. I even tried trailing him down, and camped on the trail for three nights, and eventually lost the track in a muskeg region. It was nearing spring, and I had about decided that I was beaten. I ran out of meat at that time and went about two miles from camp and put out a dozen snares for rabbits. What I did not want for food would make bait. In two or three days I went over to the rabbit snares and in the first one I looked at was a fisher. Later, I learned that this was the animal I had so persistently sought with my best methods. He had two toes missing from the front foot.

The town of Clare was a rocky region with timber in the valleys. Among the rock crevices and caves were many dens of night roamers. It was early fall and I was seeking foxes, placing them in pens to become prime. Near the base of a bluff was a seam that extended far back into the rock. The entrance was plenty large enough for a fox, and while there was but little soft material to leave sign, yet the rock seemed worn by passing feet. A trapper does not often make a fox set at a den entrance, but in this rock section, I had previously found that this type of set would bring results. It was a hard place to make a set for an elusive animal, but I sifted a leaf covering over the trap, knowing that the breezes often left leaves around such entrances. When next visiting the set I could hear the trap-chain rattling, long before I reached the set. Surely, I thought, a fox is fast, no more to roam the hills and valleys he knew as home. There was always a chance of course that a set would draw a blank in the way of some trapline pest. But I never expected to find what was caught, for with its tail tightly pinched between the steel paws of a 3XK, was a giant snake of the adder variety. And I hadn't been partaking of any liquid fire previously.

I was hunting deer in the foothills of a mountainous region, and as usual, I took a few traps with me just to make the trip interesting. The hunting was good, and the second day I came in contact with three does and two bucks that were feeding on beech nuts on the side of a hill. Right here I filled my license, which gave me time to try the trapping game for a few days. Fox and otter were the main fur-bearers and the next forenoon I went into a swamp section which was drained by a narrow stream and looked for signs of otter. In the soft mud at an elbow, I found a nice trail and set a pair of powerful traps. At an extremely narrow spot in the stream, I set another. That afternoon I put out some fox traps. Around a small hill was an animal trail, apparently used at some remote period by deer, but no fresh tracks were in evidence. Surely, I thought, this is a good set location, and selecting a number 4 trap which I had intended using for otter, I concealed it and cut a limb and fastened the trap by driving it through the trap ring into the ground until it became flush. A piece of sod over the end concealed the fastening. I do not usually fasten traps solid, but did so at this time on account of using the larger trap than was necessary. It rained that night and I was quite sure of a fox, knowing that all scent would be washed away. But there's many a slip, and when I arrived at the set a nice fat sheep was struggling in the trap. The leg was not broken nor injured seriously, and I turned it loose to wander back into the valley where the rest of the flock was grazing.

In a marsh along the Saint Lawrence River I had traps out for mink and 'rats. One morning a 'rat had been killed in a trap and partly eaten. "A mink's work," I thought, and placed a trap close by in the shallow water. On the next trip, the carcass was gone and the trap sprung. Skinning out another one I threw this down and re-set the trap. Next morning the bait had been taken again and the trap had not been molested. Things were now getting interesting, and placing fresh bait, I concealed a half dozen traps near by, using extreme care that they were covered perfectly. On the next trip, I heard a terrible squealing before I reached the sets, and rushing up, found a curious looking animal. It was apparently a cross between a mink and a weasel. It was about the size of a small mink and had the feet of this animal, but the head was more pointed, and the fur was spotted with white. I have always been sorry that I did not have this animal mounted.

## CHAPTER XXII

### UNDER ICE AND OTHER TRAPPING

IN mid-winter when the ponds, lakes and streams are frozen, many of the trapping fraternity, hug the hot stoves and wait for warm weather to start the fur-bearers moving. To make a successful trapper one must be out in every part of the season. I have heard trappers say at this time of year: "What's the use of going over my trapline when every trap is frozen down." This sounded foolish to me, realizing that if a trapline was not in catching condition, it certainly needed immediate attention to put it right.

Many northern animals move about under the ice during very cold weather, and it is only necessary to have a general knowledge of these movements to bring in a nice lot of pelts when the fur is at its best.

The laws of many states do not allow trapping for certain fur-bearers until the ice has formed. Muskrats are one of these fur-bearers. The under-ice 'rat trapper should prospect his trapping grounds before freeze-up. When a good den or den entrance is located, it should be marked so that it can be located later, but in such a way that others will not recognize the mark. After the ice forms and the season is in, a hole may be chopped in a position that a trap may be placed where it will make a catch, and no "wring-offs" or "twist-outs" will bother the trapper. Few sneakums will be operating at this time also, and one can visit his sets with a feeling of security in the belief that the catch will be awaiting him.

In the marsh-lands one should locate the tunnels where the animals move from one section to the other. Sometimes these will show up through the ice if it is of the clear variety. A trap placed in the bottom of one of these tunnels is in a fair position to nab a 'rat. If the water is more than six inches deep, the tunnel should be filled in with a stone or block of wood to raise the trap to the desired level. After making sets through a hole in the ice, the hole should be covered with a block of hard snow or other covering. This will save chopping it each time the trap is visited. I have known trappers to take a half dozen 'rats from one trap in a day, where they were moving about frequently.

A few feet back from a 'rat house the entrance may be located. Here a hole should be cut and a trap inserted. The animals move about on the bottom of the water close to a house, and a trap or two or more of them set at this place makes a fair set.

Traps set for 'rats under the ice may be fastened by shoving a pointed stick through the trap ring and into the mud at the bottom. Care should be exercised that the stick is not placed in the "run," as it may shy the animals to one side. I prefer a somewhat larger trap for under ice 'rat trapping than for other kinds, as it sometimes has to function under difficulties, such as a deep covering of mud or chewed grasses.

Beaver may be trapped in much the same manner as mentioned for muskrat, excepting the traps must be larger. Bait sets will work for beaver also. Cut a rather large hole in the ice where beaver are known to exist, and where the water is not more than three feet deep. If there is some space between the ice and water it is better. Then place in pieces of small poplar or alder saplings. These should be shoved into the bottom slightly so that the current if any, will not move them. Then a powerful trap should be set on each side of the bait. They may be fastened as suggested for 'rats, only firmer, and the trapped animal will drown quickly if the hole is allowed to freeze over. The ice chips should be removed so as to leave the spot looking natural, unless the ice is much clouded.

Otter travel about a great deal under the ice. In fact they often spend a month without ever appearing in the open. On a small trout stream is the mostly likely place to look for one. Usually the water will be higher when the ice first freezes than at a later date. This leaves a space under the ice, and often there are spots of land or a stone above water. If such can be located, a fish should be thrown upon it so as to look as if it had been frozen and lodged there. Then about three large traps should be set in the water surrounding it. Fasten in the same manner as suggested for beaver. If no natural object is found to place the bait upon, it may be impaled on a stick which must not be taken from a green tree or freshly cut.

Where the stream has been fenced off in the fall as mentioned in another chapter, the trap may be placed in the right position easily by chopping a

EVERGREENS IN WINTER

hole. A belt axe will suffice for the chopping operations.

Mink work about under shallow ice where there is an air space, and also tunnel around under the snow. Cut a hole close to the bank, and if there is any land between the water and ice, reach in and scoop out some earth so that there will be an inch of water or more reaching to the edge of the ice. Then place a trap in this dug out spot and fasten under the ice with the chain under water. Sometimes a tunnel will be located where the mink travel through. A trap placed in the tunnel and dry snow sifted or brushed over it will sometimes make a catch.

Bait in the form of a 'rat carcass or other flesh may be used under the ice for mink. To make a good bait set at this time, chop through close to a tree. If any of the washed out roots are above water, fasten the bait to this and set the trap in the water, about six inches to one side, or better still, set one on each side.

Trifling details have much to do with a perfect under-ice set or any other kind of a set. If a person visits a trap for a few trips without making a catch when he has reason to believe that the animal is working about, he should investigate and check up on the set to see what is wrong. It may be that the covering is insufficient or some obstruction may be lodged under the pan of the trap. A part of the chain may be in evidence or the clog may be too obvious. A fox or other sly animal will sometimes come within a few feet of the set and then shy directly away. There is something wrong when this happens, and one should study out and learn by his mistakes as much as he would by his successes.

Specialization sometimes pays better in the vocation of trapping than general trapping. If a trapper lives where there are many foxes it will pay him to study their habits exclusively. It takes many years to make an expert fox trapper. If a trapper divides his time between a dozen kinds of animals, he will never live long enough to learn everything about them all.

Animals like the skunk and muskrat are easier taken and trappers pursuing these will be able to successfully cope with at least a half dozen kinds. A trapper who has learned how to take any particular animal in plentiful numbers will do well to stick to this kind of trapping. This only applies from the standpoint of greater profits. If one can afford it, it is an interesting life to try out every available kind.

It does not pay any trapper to use dead-falls or other old-fashioned methods of taking furs. When animals were very plentiful they worked all right, especially as there was nothing better at that time. Box traps are only useful for taking animals alive. Snares will work fairly well for some fur-bearers, as stated in other chapters. I have known animals to be taken by boring a hole in a log or stump with a large auger and then placing bait at the back end which should be at least six inches in the wood. Then a row of horseshoe nails should be driven around the edge of the hole, with the points slanting in. When any animal shoves its head into the hole to get the bait, it will be unable to withdraw it. This is rather a dangerous trap to use, for if a person forgets and shoves his arm into the hole, he too will stay there unless he has implements for withdrawing the nails close at hand.

All traps should be tended regularly, both from a humane standpoint and on account of the pelts saved. An animal that gets free from a trap, invariably gets infection and dies. Pelts that lay too long, especially in water, are apt to be tainted and sell below their former value. Sneakums are apt to be over your line each day, so I say again: "Visit your traps as early each morning as possible."

Be square with any landowners that you come in contact with. Put up their fences instead of cutting or tearing them down and treat them as you would be treated. It will pay.

# CHAPTER XXIII

## THE CARE AND MARKETING OF FURS INCLUDING "HOME TANNING"

### CARE INCREASES VALUE

MILLIONS of dollars are wasted each year by improper and careless methods of caring for furs and skins. Animals are hard to catch, and much labor is involved in taking them, therefore one should put the skin in the best possible condition. Much poorly handled fur thrown upon a market tends to lower the price of even the better goods, so it is all-important to stretch, skin, flesh, and cure every skin properly.

It is not always the amateur that mis-handles furs. I have looked at large lots of skins that were taken by one trapper that were worth only two-thirds their true value on account of improper care. When I mentioned this fact to the trapper, he said: "Well, I didn't have time to take the best care of them, for I had to spend the most of my time on the trapline." This is poor philosophy from a remunerative standpoint.

A sharp knife is the first essential of proper care of furs. No matter how good a knife may be, it is of little use unless sharp. The nose, eyes, and ears of the animal should be cut around carefully, not leaving great holes to mar the skin. On animals like mink, the claws should be left on the skin. All dealers do not demand this, but some do, and they do no harm.

Stretchers should be smooth and uniform. No animal should be overstretched, as this tends to thin up the fur when it has to cover a greater surface. All skins are judged as much or more by the quality of fur than by the size.

Furs should always be cured in a well ventilated room. A rather dark place is preferred as the direct rays of the sun are detrimental to the skin. Furs should never be placed on a stretcher until thoroughly dry. Nearly all water animals are taken from the traps in a drowned and wet condition. These should be hung in an airy place until dry and fluffed out.

The tail bones of every animal should be removed and the skin split to the point. All fat and pieces of flesh should be scraped off with a dull knife. A little salt on the tail and feet will aid in curing, but it should never be placed on the body.

Skins that are to be summered over, should be thoroughly dried and packed in alternate layers of cedar leaves.

### MARKETING

Some trappers ship their furs to city dealers, and others sell to local dealers who in turn ship to large cities. Both these methods have their advantages. When selling locally, one does not part with his furs, and he can get offers while his furs are on the stretchers, so to speak. Then he knows who he is selling to, and chooses a reliable dealer.

The dealers in the city are naturally better posted on up-to-the-minute market quotations, and in some instances is in position to get more for his goods than the small town dealer. But a trapper should

SOME FARMLAND FURS

never send large amounts of furs to houses he knows nothing about. Only recently, hundreds of trappers shipped furs to a fake house that paid almost nothing. This dealer was later placed in prison, but few of the trappers got their money back. Generally speaking, a fur house that quotes much more than nearly all other fur houses is conceded "crooked." All furs must ultimately find their way to the same markets, and one firm cannot pay much more than another. Of course some firms might operate on less expense, and therefore could pay a trifle more. Firms that quote many prices on one kind of fur, do so with the thought of confusing the shipper. Extra large animals are like persons of that type. We see them in circuses and shows that weigh four and five hundred pounds, but not one person in each ten thousand attain this weight. So it is with the fur-bearers.

Furs that are to be shipped long distances must be thoroughly dried before packing. They should never be rolled but packed flat. Small amounts should be sent by parcel post, and large lots by express. Avoid packing in heavy boxes or barrels as much as possible, and use burlap for wrapping.

Some skins like muskrats are often bought and sold as "flat," or at an average price. This is a very satisfactory way to sell and leaves less room for argument than when selling on a sort.

Only prime skins are wanted by dealers or manufacturers at the present time, and I hope to see the time when such furs will be the only kind purchased at any price. Furs do not reach their prime stage at the same time each year, and if the fall has been exceedingly warm, one should not start trapping operations at the usual time. Skins from animals like the skunk and 'coon may appear prime on the pelt side when caught and within a few days show much blue or black which denotes that the animal was taken too early. This often causes argument, when skins are shipped very green. When they leave the hands of the trapper they may appear as number 1 pelts, but on arrival they show their true state. Occasionally an animal will be taken in midwinter that is unprime. This is caused by poor food conditions or by sickness.

It does not pay to kill an accidental catch of a mink or other fur-bearer that may get in one's traps in the late spring when they are set for muskrat, otter or beaver. Such skins bring but a paltry sum and are apt to be females that would raise many young.

### HOME TANNING

Often a skin is taken that has many pleasant memories attached to it, or a trapper may wish to give a tanned skin to some person. In the cold climates a person may wish to tan some of his own skins for clothing.

The first operation is to get the skin scraped free of flesh and grease, and thoroughly softened. The skin must be soaked in water until soft. Do not leave more than two hours or the fur may slip. All the oil and grease may be removed from a skin by washing in gasoline. This is important.

To make a tanning solution, dissolve a pound of aluminum sulphate and one pound of salt in a small quantity of water. Then dissolve two ounces of terra japonica in a little boiling water. Mix the two solutions so as to make up two gallons. Add enough flour to make a paste. When the skins are soaked, cleaned and ready, apply a coating of the paste and roll up. If the skin is thick, clean off the paste at the end of twenty-four hours and apply another coating. Then at the end of forty-eight hours, wash off the paste and rinse in cold water. Wring out and apply a little vaseline or neat's foot oil, and while the skin is drying, work it occasionally by drawing over a taut rope or pole to make it pliable. This method is recommended by the U. S. Dept. of Agriculture, and will accomplish fine results.

A simple method is known as the salt-alum process. This solution may be made up as follows: Dissolve one pound of alum in a gallon of water, then four ounces of washing soda and eight ounces of salt in one-half gallon of water. Mix the solutions together. Flour may be added and a paste spread over the skin or it may be immersed for two days, then clean and dry as recommended previously.

A salt-acid tanning solution is made up as follows: Dissolve a pound of common salt in a gallon of water. Then add one-half ounce of sulphuric acid. This solution must be prepared and kept in wooden containers. Place the skin in this solution and let it remain for three days, when it should be washed in borax and water and dried in the manner described heretofore.

Heavy skins may be tanned by immersing in a solution of ground oak bark and water for ten days. The hair may be removed by soaking in warm water or a solution of ten pounds of hydrated lime to each four gallons of water. The hair should be scraped off. Oil or grease well before entirely dry.

Rawhide is made by simply removing the hair and cutting into strips. The Indians smoked their rawhide. It may be oiled.

## CHAPTER XXIV

### FUR FARMING

AS a side line for a trapper, I know of no better or more remunerative vocation than fur farming. A person who has followed the trail and trapline for years is in a good position to know the habits of fur-bearers in their wild state, and therefore should make successful fur farmers. Then they are usually able to collect their own stock which not only saves a great outlay of cash, but tends to get a good strain.

One should select the type of animal that he is most familiar with, and the one which is most adapted to the territory which he intends using. For instance, a marshy section will be best for the propagation of muskrats or beaver. A high, sandy region would be fine for foxes, and a timbered fur farm would be the right thing for marten or fisher. 'Coon will do well almost anywhere, but the price of the pelts are not as high as some of the others.

There are two common methods of taking live animals for ranching stock. One is by the use of box style traps, and the other by trapping with steel traps with jaws wound with cloth. Occasionally, animals may be trailed to their den and removed, being the method that takes the animals with the least harm.

For taking 'rats, there is a wire trap known as the "colony trap," that may be placed under water in the middle of a stream or in a rat "run" in the marshes, and it will take and hold any animal that swims into it. This method of setting would of course drown every 'rat that was captured. But when placed on the bank and baited with bits of flag roots or other natural food, some of these furbearers may be taken.

Few states or provinces protect fox, and these may be dug from their dens when small. This applies mostly to reds or the common colors, as the silvers and blacks are too scare in their wild state, and must be procured through another dealer. I advise that the tyro fox farmer will begin with reds which he can procure himself, and then when he has become familiar with the business, he may change to the more expensive kind.

'Coon may often be located in den trees and the tree chopped down. Those seeking the animals for their fur only, should never destroy a den of any kind.

Even the common skunk is being raised with much profit at the present time. They may be taken in box traps or by removing from the den. Only when the lawful season is in effect may they be taken. The scent glands are usually removed when the animals are young, thus making them as harmless as a house cat.

Rabbits are raised extensively for fur and meat, and considering their prolificness, considerable money may be made in a comparatively short period. Their natural food being vegetables, these may be raised by the person who owns the rabbits. When the animals are full grown, they should be fatted on grains to procure the best price. Rab-

SILVER FOX ON A FUR FARM

bits or hares as they are usually known, sell readily in New York and the big cities for as high an average as fowl, and they are easier raised. Then the skins from the better kinds often sell for twenty-five cents or more which brings the total to sometimes as high as one dollar each.

In the warm or hot weather it is advisable to ship rabbits alive to avoid the loss by the flesh spoiling in transit. Commission houses sell the meat for a small percentage, which does not necessitate the owner to visit the city with his produce.

Generally speaking, wire enclosures are used for keeping every fur-bearer. These should vary in size according to the animal, but should always be large enough to allow the animals room to properly exercise. A pen for a pair of foxes should be at least twelve feet square and larger would be better. It is not necessary to cover over the top with wire more than two feet out from the edge, unless climbing animals like marten or fisher are to be penned.

In each wire enclosure an enclosed den should be made of lumber or other material. This should have a winding entrance, and be constructed with a door at the top to allow cleaning or inspection.

During the mating and breeding season of the wilder fur-bearers, strangers must not be allowed near the pens. A fox for instance, will sometimes devour her young if scared badly, or they will bury them in the ground. A few kinds will allow the handling of their young.

Around the animal pens, a large enclosure of wire is usually placed so that if by any chance one of the animals got free from their cage, the outer pen would prevent them from getting away. An observatory is often built in the middle of the yard where the animals may be watched and not molested. This should be high enough to give a clear view to all parts of the pens.

Water animals are somewhat harder to enclose, but if one has a large territory they seek and procure much of their own food, and are less liable to disease than those enclosed in smaller areas. Fine mesh wire sunk two feet or more below the earth's surface will usually suffice for keeping in water animals. Some persons do not fence their fur farm, but purchase a large tract of marsh and prevent trapping until the animals get a start. Then they trap off a percentage each year and leave plenty to breed.

A person with a marsh of five hundred acres is in position to reap a golden harvest every year, and there are such places at the present time which are considered almost valueless by the owners who do not go in for trapping, and know nothing of the hidden wealth they contain.

Food is one of the main essentials of successful fur farming. There must not only be plenty of it, but a constant variety. Many of the species do well on a meat diet, but all need other varieties of food. Experience alone will teach whether the food is better cooked or raw. Of course the animals do not get cooked food in the fields and forests, and until one learns different, he should stay as close to nature's methods as possible.

Worn out horses are generally obtainable for

the price of their hide, and horse flesh apparently agrees with many of the animals.

Cleanliness is absolutely necessary, both as to food and pen conditions. Fresh sand spread about the pens assures easy cleaning. Sawdust may be used but is not as satisfactory.

Pure drinking water is just as important as food. Good spring water is used whenever possible. It should be cool and kept in the pens at all times.

The breeder will ever try to attain better stock. Animals that realize their value by the color may often be improved by keeping only the best colors for breeders. This applies to skunk especially. The size may also be improved by using the best original stock. Many fur-bearers are now bred and sold on a "standard" basis. Animals not coming up to this standard are killed off and sold at fur values.

The northern sections are more adapted to the raising of fur-bearers on account of the better quality of fur, but even southern animals may be raised at a profit. Elevation and good air help to produce fine furs.

New York State has many hundred fur farms at the present time, and more are started each year. This means that stock is worth much more than the price of the fur, and breeders are quick sale.

Beaver are easily raised where conditions are favorable and being very hardy are not quite immune from disease, unless too closely confined. Like the 'rat, they do well in territory hardly adapted to any other use. Permits are usually necessary from the game commission of the state in which the beaver are propagated.

The fur from ranch raised animals is considered about equal with that of the animals of the wild. One can of course, kill off those intended for fur when the pelts are prime and the market in good condition. If there comes a bad year in the fur business, the fur farmer may keep his entire crop until the following year, or until the price is satisfactory.

Fur farming is not an occupation that will make one rich in a short period, for it takes considerable time to put the thing on a paying basis. I am confident however, that it is one of the great future American industries, and the person who gets in at the start is sure to eventually win out, especially if he is an energetic person and keeps conditions as near to the former environment of the animals as possible.

## CHAPTER XXV

### OUTDOOR PHOTOGRAPHY
#### CAMERAS

IN the beginning, a camera is only a light-proof box with lens placed in one end and a receptacle for holding plates or film in the other. The cheaper kinds contain little more, excepting a shutter that allows a given amount of light to pass through the lens and reflect on the sensitized surface of the plate or film. This is operated at will by the photographer and the manipulation is known as "taking the picture."

The principle of the most expensive cameras is exactly the same, but they are equipped with more conveniences and are adapted to a wider scope of work. The lens may be operated with a larger opening in the shutter, and the speed of the shutter is more varied and rapid than the cheaper kinds.

There are three kinds of lens commonly used on cameras. The cheapest kinds have a single lens known as an achromatic, meaning transmitting light without decomposition. The medium priced instruments have what is known as rectilinear lens, having the power of rendering straight lines straight. The best cameras are equipped with anastigmat lens, which the light in passing through does not deviate from a given path. This lens has all the advantages of the others and will work at much faster speed without distortion. The best lens of the type just mentioned operates at the stop in the shutter known as F:4. At this opening snapshots may be made without sunlight, hence one can make rapid pictures in shade such as the trapper encounters in the backwoods. Speedy lenses are better for photographing live wild animals, for they are constantly moving about, and a slow lens would record the movement on the finished negative and print.

The size of a camera will depend on the work to be done and the individual needs of the photographer. Small sizes with good lens will produce negatives that will enlarge perfectly and are much easier carried than bulky ones. The folding kinds are the only thing to be considered for a trapper or hunter who is usually loaded down with equipment. Roll film is more easily procured than plates or film packs, yet a real photographer will want a machine that he can focus the image on a ground glass at the back. With roll film, this is impossible, excepting on a few bulky types like a graflex.

### EXPOSURE

Let us assume that we are about to make a photograph. Suppose it is slightly cloudy, and we are making a scene with dark background. If we are using a folding hand camera without a ground glass, we locate the scene in the view finder and swing the instrument back and forth until we get the right composition. More or less sky can be had by tilting the camera to a different angle. If tall trees or other objects are close by, the camera should be held level. The better grades have a spirit level on them for this purpose. For portraits or close up views of animals the camera may be tilted to get the image as wished. When the view finder shows that the picture will appear as you wish it, see that the focusing device is set in the proper notch to correspond with the distance you are working at. Then note that your film is rolled to a fresh number, or if packs are used, that a tab has been removed. Then set the shutter at the fastest speed the light will stand, being about 1-25 of a second with a lens working at F:7.7, which will give a fully timed negative with light clouds. Other speeds will vary accordingly. For every stop on a shutter the time should be doubled, beginning at the largest and continuing to the smallest.

For time exposure, every camera should be placed on a firm support like a good tripod. This method of exposing gives better results on objects that do not move rapidly. If the light is so bright that any exposure of the time variety, being slower than 1-25 of a second, would over-expose, then one must use a smaller stop in the shutter, which will give a sharper focus and a correspondingly sharper image on the negative. The more expensive instruments have automatic shutters that make time exposures with one pressure of the release. Others must be set at T, and the release worked once to open and once to close. For outdoor subjects, with a medium stop, one cannot open and close the shutter too quickly to give correct exposure unless the object is in dense shade or the light is very poor. Remember that during the period that the shutter is open, that a slight movement will ruin the finished picture. Bulb exposures are much the same as a time exposure, excepting the shutter remains open as long as the bulb or finger release is pressed. It closes automatically when the pressure is ceased.

PHOTOGRAPH OF A LADY TRAPPER WITH A DEER SHE KILLED

Exposure meters may be purchased cheaply, which has a complete table of every light condition and every opening in shutters. These are very good for amateurs and some professionals use them at all times.

Work to make your exposures as equal as possible. This will enable the film to be developed with better results, as nearly all finishers give the whole roll or pack the same time in the developer, and if a good many different exposures are used the finished product will not be uniform.

#### PHOTOGRAPHING WILD ANIMALS

Care and patience are among the factors of a good animal photographer. Not given to posing, the wild creatures usually begin making contortions of every description when brought in front of a camera. One of the main essentials is to pose the subject amid natural surroundings. A 'rat would never look natural unless a stream or other water were in the background, and a skunk on the shore of a river would look out of place, even though they do visit such places occasionally.

Be sure that the animal is the right distance from the camera, or if a ground glass is used, focus sharply, for with the usual movements, the largest stop and a quick exposure is quite necessary.

Some photographers make photos of very wild creatures by fastening a tiny string to the shutter release and then hiding some distance from the camera. If deer, moose, or other animals have a habit of drinking at a certain spot during the time when the light is bright enough for an exposure, one can often get a photo by the method just described. Sometimes one can run a deer down on snowshoes when the snow is very deep, and a photo can then be made.

A small attachment for cameras known as a "tripper," will make the exposure at a given time in an automatic manner. This allows one to get in the picture himself, or to aid in posing the subject. When photographing small animals or subjects like birds, squirrels, fish, etc., one should use an extra lens known as a portrait lens, and which slips over the regular lens, unless the camera has a very long bellows, which allows the photographer to focus sharply at very close range. Otherwise the image will be so small that it will hardly be recognized on the finished picture.

### REMARKS

It is commonly thought that one must stand with the sun at his back when making an exposure. This is not essential and in some instances ruins the effect. Light coming from one side is usually better, or if facing the lens, they should be shaded with a hat, slide from a plateholder, or a piece of paper. None of these objects should be in range of the lens.

Photographs of lightning may be made at night by opening the shutter, placing in position with the lens facing the storm, and awaiting a flash. When it comes, close the shutter. Photographs with true color values may be made by using a device known as a ray filter. This slips over the regular lens, and while using it, the exposure should be doubled.

The outdoorsman should learn to finish his own photographs for often he will be far back in the wilderness for long periods, which would tend to ruin the unfinished film. The fundamentals of photo finishing are very simple and the whole necessary equipment weighs but a trifle. Of course when one has to back-pack in everything, he will probably forego the finishing articles and take a chance on his film spoiling.

It is often possible to sell good photographs of outdoor subjects. Magazines, books, and papers all need photographs, and the publishers often pay well for them. They must be sharp, however, and the composition good. A few moments spent in composing the subject when the photo is made will more than pay when it is sold. Photographs for reproduction should be made on glossy paper and should show only a medium amount of contrast.

Advertisers often purchase photographs of articles made by them in actual use in the outdoors. Guns, traps and all hunting and trapping equipment come under this. A trapper can often pay his expenses by carrying a small camera of a good type.

# CONCLUSION

VISIONS of the trapline and trail come drifting back in fond memory. Again I see the great, snow-capped summits of a majestic mountain range in front of a little log cabin. It is early morning and a pinkish glow shows far beyond the tip of old Panther peak. Then as I seemingly stand in front of the cabin, the sun bursts forth from back of the mighty range, kissing the spruce filled valley with its radiant light. The leafless hardwoods stand out in bold contrast against the background of evergreens, which bedecked with particles of hoar-frost, scintillate in the morning light like innumerable jewels.

Then after a day on the trapline, with its mysteries, uncertainties, and countless thrills, I stand near the summits of the same range, and the vision is reversed. Far down in the silent valley, I can distinguish the outline of the little cabin I knew as "Home." Perhaps the partner is in camp, and a wisp of bluish-white smoke curls skyward, being the only sign of human existence away to the very skyline of spruce. The little brook that rippled past the cabin in summer, is frozen and buried under a carpet of snow, but farther down at the falls I can hear the roar of angry waters, their euphonic rhythm sounding wonderfully sweet to the tired but happy trapper.

Visions of nights in the cabin come back, when the fur was stretched by the flickering candle light. The huge box stove filled with birch, whistled and

E. J. DAILEY WITH "GO LIGHT CAMPING OUTFIT"

spurted flame as it burned. Then the skillet was brought forth and filled with choice venison steak for the bed-time lunch. And after this was eaten, the pipes were filled and events of the day discussed. Perhaps the partner tells of an animal getting away into the deep forest with the trap and clog. Then a chase ensued and a trail worked out. Perhaps a snarling 'cat was found in some sheltering tree, with the steel dog still clinging to its toes. Or it may have been a giant fox tangled in the brush. Tales of wise fur-bearers that are constantly eluding sets, but which one hopes to find fast on the next trip, are common. Strange tracks are always discussed, and fresh arrivals of the animal family on the trapping ground. Surely, "this is a man's life."

There are hardships and dangers attached to a far back trapline. The elements of the north are hard to battle. Yet the worth while joys bury the hardships deep, where they seldom resurrect themselves in memory.

Dreams of autumn days along the trapline of the farmlands are only too fond. I can see the crimson and gild of the scattered woodlands, and hear the "cawing" of the countless crows hastening away on their southern flight. At early morn as I saunter across the meadows, I quicken my pace, for over at the gapway in the old, tumble-down stonewall, a fox trap has been carefully concealed. Then along the sugar-woods are skunk sets, and one hopes for a striped beauty at that point. A whistling plowboy leisurely makes his way to work, with much rattle of heavy trace chains, as they extend from the hips of rugged plow-beasts. The autumn haze extends away to the hills, and the air has a hollow sound, with echoes reverberating for many miles. No king on his throne has more than this.

---

The foregoing is my answer to a question I know many readers would like to ask: "Do you advise me to become a trapper?" If you are not a lover of the outdoors, brother, you never would make a successful trapper, for trapping is much more than a chance to eke out a precarious living, at least from the writer's viewpoint.

In this book I have tried not to stray from facts. I realize that some persons may disagree with some of my statements, realizing that occasionally what applies in one section might not prove worthy in another. I sincerely believe that the information given will cover every territory in a general way. Personally, I have tried nearly every method given, and know they will bring results. Some of the information given in this book was gleaned from nomadic trappers who have spent nearly their entire life among the fur-bearers, in nature-favored spots of the wild. Methods given have been told to me, many scores of miles from civilization, and in front of smoldering camp-fires in the open forest. Some were given by inmates of caves, earth houses and hardy persons that braved the rigors of a northern winter in open camps.

Before bringing the book to a close, I want to ask the readers once more "To play fair with the wild things, and give them a chance to replenish the earth with their species."

# The Wilderness Trapper

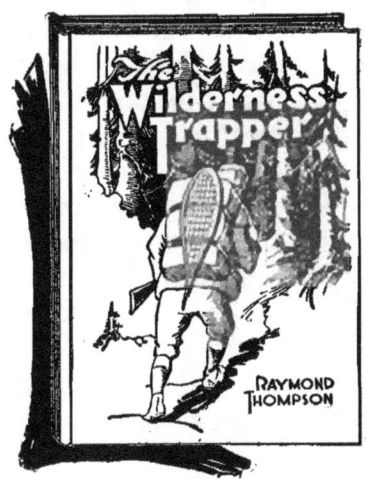

A manual on trapping, by Raymond Thompson, who has spent many years on the wilderness trapline. There are sixteen chapters of practical information on trapping, instructive and interesting. A valuable guide book. Some of the chapters are on: Outfitting the Wilderness Trapper; The Grub Stake; Getting Ready for the Fur Harvest; Fox Trapping; War on Wolves; Beaver Trapping; The Lynx; Marten and Fisher Trapping; The Bear Family; Muskrat; Tracks and Tracking; Grading Furs; Caring for Steel Traps; Firearms and Snowshoes, etc.

This interesting book contains 226 pages, with numerous pictures and drawings of sets and tracks. Cloth bound, only $1.00.

PUBLISHED BY
**THE HUNTER - TRADER - TRAPPER COMPANY**
COLUMBUS, OHIO, U. S. A.

# The River Trapper

By Walter S. Chansler.

*A Treatise on The Life of a Houseboat Dweller and His River Wanderings*

Actual experiences of the Author in his Houseboat, depicting the coves and bayous along the rivers, lucky escapes, and profitable pursuits in fishing, trapping, mussel and root gathering.

A Book you will want to read. Published by H-T-T. This book is cloth bound, contains 214 pages, 15 chapters and 28 illustrations of interesting scenes along the route.

PRICE ONLY $1.00 POST PAID

PUBLISHED BY
## HUNTER-TRADER-TRAPPER
Columbus, Ohio, U. S. A.

# Cooning With Cooners

*Packed With Real Coon Hunting Experiences.
Illustrated From Typical Photographs*

A favorite book for every coon hunter. Compiled by O. Kuechler, Editor of Hunter-Trader-Trapper, and containing many interesting stories of actual coon hunts with coon hunting dogs. Stories similar to those published monthly in the Coon Hunting Department of H-T-T. This book should be in the home of every lover of the sport.

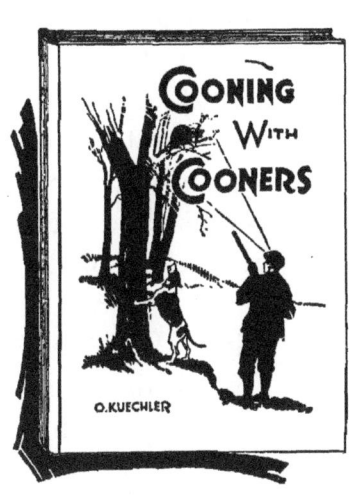

Cloth bound, 217 pages.   Price $1.00.

PUBLISHED BY

**THE HUNTER - TRADER - TRAPPER COMPANY**
COLUMBUS, OHIO, U. S. A.

# "Fighting Red Cloud's Warriors"

### The Frontier Series — Vol. II

## True Tales of Indian Days When the West Was Young

$1.00 Only;
Prepaid

Ten chapters of authentic information of Buffalo days and Indian fights. Real live literature of frontier happenings. No fiction. Embellished with 44 rare illustrations of the battle fields and men taking parts in "The Tragedy of Fort Phil Kearney", "The Wagon Box Fight", the "Buffalo Wallow Fight", and other noted encounters.

This book contains 241 pages, cloth bound, and sells for only $1.00, postpaid.

PUBLISHED BY

**THE HUNTER - TRADER - TRAPPER COMPANY**

COLUMBUS, OHIO, U. S. A.

# A Book on the Coon Hound, --- Exclusively ---

"Training a Coonhound," presenting right methods to meet various conditions; "Proper Breeding," facts you should know and be guided by to get the best results. "Care of Puppies" from birth to doghood, also what and when to feed them; "Cross Breeding" and the results usually obtained; "Inbreeding" defined and its results explained; "Dog Diseases," their causes, cures and prevention; "The Glossary", defining the anatomy of a dog and explaining terms used with reference to the chase.

Cloth bound, 5¼x7½, 160 pages, good readable type, fully illustrated with interesting pictures from different sections of the country. Price only $1.00 prepaid.

**PUBLISHED BY**
**THE HUNTER - TRADER - TRAPPER COMPANY**
COLUMBUS, OHIO, U. S. A.

# Hunter-Trader-Trapper

### The Largest Outdoor Magazine of Its Kind in the World

Fully illustrated with photos of actual happenings on the trap line, in the field, along the lakes and streams, etc. From 96 to 160 pages in each issue, every page full of human interest. Published every month in the year.

If you have never seen a copy, send us 25c and we will be glad to forward one, postpaid. A whole year only $2.00.

## HUNTER-TRADER-TRAPPER
### COLUMBUS, OHIO, U. S. A.

# Training the Rabbit Hound

Carl Smith the author has had many years experience in the breeding and training of rabbit dogs. While his pet breed is the Basset nevertheless the beagle is given his full share of comment in this new book. The training methods of course can be applied to any dog suitable for rabbit hunting. The same can be said of the chapter on diseases and remedies. No matter what kind of a dog you own you can't go wrong in buying this book.

It is fully illustrated with famous rabbit hounds on the bench and also in action. Bound in cloth with front cover as illustrated and the same size as all other books published by H-T-T. Only $1.00 Prepaid.

PUBLISHED BY
**THE HUNTER - TRADER - TRAPPER COMPANY**
COLUMBUS, OHIO, U. S. A.

VOLUME I—FRONTIER SERIES.

# A Trooper With Custer

## BY E. A. BRININSTOOL.

*Gripping Facts of Custer's Last Fight. Every character a participant in the making of the West. No fiction.*

**Gripping Facts About Frontier Fighting**

**Price $1.00 only Postpaid**

Eleven chapters of thrilling details of the greatest Indian battle ever fought on the American continent, the famous "Battle of the Little Big Horn." Stories by actual participants and survivors of Major Reno's command; startling, sensational testimony at Reno Court of Inquiry; miraculous escape of Slaper, Lieut. De Rudio, Sergt. O'Neill and others. Photographs of priceless value are used for illustrations. It contains 214 pages, cloth bound, and should be owned by every red-blooded American.

PUBLISHED BY
**THE HUNTER-TRADER-TRAPPER COMPANY**
COLUMBUS, OHIO, U. S. A.

# Fishermen All!

## You want a copy of "Sam" Camp's New Book

**Send $1.00 only**

### Part of Contents

**Fly Tackle for Trout and Bass.**
Fly rods—Selecting the fly rod—The fly rod for bass—Steel fly rods—Care of rods—The fly casting reel—The fly casting line—Leaders—Dry and wet fly terminal tackle—Advantages of the single fly—Trout flies—Fly books and boxes—Bass flies—Fly rod lures for bass and trout.

**Trout and Trout Fishing Methods.**
Fly casting—Wet fly fishing—The dry fly method—Pan fishing with dry fly—Early fly fishing—Striking, playing and landing—Worm fishing for trout.

**Bait Casting for Bass and Others: Fly Rod Fishing.**
Casting rods—Casting reels—Lines—Bait casting and casting baits (How to cast; habits of bass and other game fish; casting lures; etc.)—Playing and landing—Practical hints—Fly rod fishing.

**Trolling; Still Fishing; Pan Fishing.**
Trolling tackle, baits and methods—How to distinguish pike, pickerel and muskellunge—Still fishing tackle and methods—Pan fishing—How to distinguish the rock bass, calico bass and crappie—Tackle—"Perch bugs"—Where to fish—Trolling and casting.

### A SOUND BOOK BY AN AUTHORITY

Mr. Camp has been a nationally recognized authority on angling for nearly twenty years. This is his latest and best book—a practical handbook, covering all essential phases of fresh-water fishing. Written in his usual entertaining style. Fully illustrated, from photographs and drawings. Over 200 pages.

**PUBLISHED BY**

## THE HUNTER - TRADER - TRAPPER COMPANY
### COLUMBUS, OHIO, U. S. A.

CPSIA information can be obtained
at www.ICGtesting.com
Printed in the USA
LVHW051311170221
679367LV00029B/211